I dedicate t

I also want t͟ ͟ ͟ ͟ ͟ ͟ ͟nd
friends who h͟ ͟ ͟ ͟ ͟ ͟ ͟e on my journey
and shared with me their love, friendship,
support, kindness and sense of humour every
step of the way. Special mention also to my
friends in the armed forces who simply leave
me humbled.

Finally, this book is also dedicated to my
fantastic huskies, Harley and Max!

No Worries

by Gary 'Smiler' Turner

First edition, first printing

Published by Gary Turner

Copyright © Gary Turner, 2013, England

All rights reserved. This publication may not be copied or reproduced in whole or in part by any means or in any manner whatsoever without the written permission of the author.

The author's personal website is:
www.garyturner.co.uk

1

Good News!   6

Nice To Meet You!   7

About This Book   9

Fact File 1: Understand Anxiety   13
   Relax And Read   13
   How Feelings Arise   13
   How Anxiety Arises   16
   Fear Serves A Purpose   18
   Anxiety And Related Issues   23
   Applying The Knowledge   26

Fact File 2: Understand Your Mind   31
   Learning To Change   31
   Stimulus And Response   31
   Perception And Reality   33
   Memories Are Plastic   34
   A Learned Fear   36

ACT 1: Calm your mind   41
   Starting To Change   41
   Step 2: Playing With Feelings   44
   The Magic Of Imagination   48

ACT 2: Distract Your Mind   55
   The Four-legged Therapist   55
   Using Distraction   56
   Step 3: Body And Mind   58
   Step 4: Music Magic   59
   Step 5: Positive Attention   61

Matt's Story: No More Travel Troubles!   64

ACT 3: Relax Yourself   67
   Relaxation Matters   67
   How To Relax   67
   Why Closed Eyes?   68
   Step 6: Deep Relaxation   68

Liz's Story: No More Rage And Sleep Problems!	73
ACT 4: Use Non-anxious Language	**77**
Anxiety And Language	77
The Power Of Certainty	78
Step 7: Avoiding Anxious Language	79
Practising Positive Language	82
Naomi's Story: No More Public Speaking Panic!	85
ACT 5: Change Your Critical Voice	**87**
Your Internal Voice	87
Your Critical Voice	87
The Quick Fix	88
Step 8: CV Change – Sound	89
Pronoun Replacement	91
Step 9: CV Change – Location	92
Step 10: CV Change – Urgency	93
Test Yourself	96
Susan's Story: No More Workplace Woes!	99
ACT 6: Create Your Positive Voice	**101**
Personality And Voices	101
Step 11: CV Change – Gag It!	101
Step 12: CV Change – Comfort It!	102
Step 13: CV Change – Direct It!	104
Anthony's Story: No More Flying Fears!	107
ACT 7: Escape Your Past	**109**
Healing Emotions	109
Programmed By Your Past	109
Step 14: Memory Extension	110
Step 15: Deleting Negative Emotion	113
Step 16: Fixing The Past	115
Jim's Story: No More Sleep Struggles!	119
ACT 8: Direct Your Future	**121**
Future Memories	121
Step 17: The Day After	121
Step 18: From Then To Now	123

Step 19: Mental Rehearsal	125
Step 20: Seeing The Future	126
Anne's Story: No More Spoiled Sport!	**130**
A Simple Request	**131**
ACT 9: Put It All Together!	**133**
An Interesting Journey	133
Step 21: Put It All Together	133
Conclusion 136	
Acknowledgements	**137**
Recommended Reading	**139**

"He's turned his life around. He used to be depressed and miserable. Now he's miserable and depressed."

– Harry Kalas

Good News!

You want some good news?

Here's plenty!

You *can* overcome whatever problem you have with anxiety, worry or nerves.

You *can* live the rest of your life without any anxiety issues whatsoever.

I *can* guarantee it!

I know that anxiety can be a terrible, persistent, difficult problem. I sympathise, and I'm not saying you will get rid of the problem overnight or with a simple click of the fingers. It will take a little bit of effort and a little bit of time.

But you *will* get there, and live the rest of your life utterly, totally free from unnecessary anxiety, nerves, worry or stress.

This book will tell you everything you need to know, and give you all the help you need to get rid of anxiety problems forever.

As you go on your journey through this book, you will learn a great deal about yourself, your mind and your body. You will discover how to change just about anything you want about who you are and how you live your life. It's actually pretty fascinating stuff!

By the time we get to the end, not only will you be free from anxiety, you will know how to bring about any other personal change you want as well.

Does that sound good?

Okay!

Let's get started…

Nice To Meet You!

Since we're going on this journey together, I thought I'd just say hello and introduce myself.

There are a lot of people around who will say they can help you overcome stress and anxiety. So what makes me different? Not much, except that in my case I *had* to learn how to overcome anxiety in order to stay alive! I know that sounds a little melodramatic and 'over the top', but it's very close to the truth.

I had quite a successful career as a professional athlete and sportsman, winning over a dozen world titles in various fighting sports. When I was competing, there was no room for anxiety and worry, because an anxious fighter usually loses! I had to learn how to be calm, focused and positive. That's how I first became fascinated by the whole question of how to overcome anxiety.

These days, most of my work is in clinical hypnosis and related fields. I help people to overcome their fears, anxieties, phobias and addictions, and I *love* this work! I consider it a privilege to work with each and every one of my clients, just as I consider it a privilege now to work with you, my dear reader!

I'm often referred to as Gary 'Smiler' Turner, for the simple reason that I *do* actually smile a lot! I think it's just because I enjoy life, enjoy meeting new people and enjoy all the opportunities that life brings. In my years as a professional sportsman, I even used to smile through the bouts that were definitely *not* going my way. Why? Because I still enjoyed them! I was still competing at the highest level, exploring my potential and learning how to be the best I could be.

My work takes me all over the UK and sometimes overseas. However, I live in the south of England with my lovely wife Kirsty and my two huskies, Max and Harley.

Did I Mention Fighting?

I mentioned that I used to compete professionally in various fighting sports. I know that for many of you, the word 'fight' has negative associations: violence, conflict, thugs and aggressive people you want to stay away from.

Let me be clear: I am the *least* violent person you will ever meet. In fact, unless you've got plans to meet Gandhi or Buddha later on today, I'm probably the closest you'll ever get to Mr. Peace and Sunshine. I *never* behave in an aggressive or violent way. I always conduct myself in a polite, peaceful and respectful way, and no-one in the world despises violence or aggression more than I do.

I can assure you that if I ever, for one moment, displayed any aggressive tendencies, my lovely wife Kirsty would call me an idiot (quite rightly) pack her bags and be off. (In our home there's only room for one person to be the boss, call the shots and lay down the law... and it's her.)

Fighting sports are not about hurting people. They are about training, strength, discipline, technique, speed and stamina. The guy who wins the bout isn't the brutal thug. He won't last for ten seconds. It's the guy who has trained and worked hard to be faster, smarter and quicker so he can *avoid* being hit, and who can outclass the other guy based on speed, tactics, quickness of mind and just enough strength and stamina to win the contest.

For me, these sports were about the discipline of being as fit as I could possibly be – in mind, body and spirit.

So if the word 'fighting' has caused you to raise your eyebrow and wonder if I'm really someone whose book you want to read, let me reassure you: I totally condemn all forms of violence and aggression. Anyone who behaves aggressively towards another person is a loser in my eyes, and I will have nothing to do with them.

About This Book

This is not a 'self-help' book. I am going to be with you every step of the way. I am going on the journey with you.

In my work as a professional hypnotherapist, I have helped countless men and women from all walks of life to overcome their anxiety issues, and to overcome them forever. I do this using a simple, safe and *enjoyable* approach that I call ACT (Anxiety Clearing Technique). In this book, I will take you through the same ACT approach — the one that has already helped thousands of people to successfully overcome anxiety forever. It worked for them, and it will work for you.

How It Works

If you tend to suffer from anxiety issues, you probably already feel a bit anxious about *this book itself*, and what 'getting rid of the problem' will actually *involve!*

So, let me explain exactly what's going to happen. It's simple, safe and enjoyable.

First of all, I'm going to help you to understand what anxiety really is — how it arises, and how it affects your body and mind.

Secondly, I will explain in general terms how you can overcome anxiety issues of any kind, and deal with them effectively so they are never a problem ever again.

Thirdly, I'll take you through the Anxiety Clearing Technique (ACT) that I mentioned above. This is just a series of exercises that you do in your mind. There's no hypnosis, and there's nothing weird about it. Think of it as like a visit to a spa, except instead of soothing and massaging the muscles of your body, you will be learning to soothe and massage the patterns in your mind. It's actually very peaceful and relaxing!

And that's all there is to it.

Welcome to the new you, free from anxiety issues forever.

How To Use The Steps

'ACT' stands for Anxiety Clearing Technique. There are nine stages, called ACT 1, ACT 2 and so on.

Each ACT involves one or more steps, which are sort of like mental exercises or games. They're all easy to do.

There are 21 steps in this book overall. I know that sounds like a lot, but I promise it isn't really. Most of the steps are very short. You will have reached the end of this book before you even know it!

When you come to each step, please use them as follows.

- Make sure you have enough time, and enough peace and quiet, to use each step properly and gain the full benefit. You don't need total seclusion and silence. You just need a bit of time to yourself and freedom from distractions.

- Read the instructions two or three times before you actually use each step. This will imprint on your mind what you need to be doing and make the steps much more effective.

- When I ask you to imagine something, please imagine it to the very best of your ability. Imagine it clearly, vividly and in as much detail as possible. Make the images in your mind large, bold, clear and colourful. Imagine them so completely that they are as real as they can be in your mind. Your imagination is an amazingly powerful gift — please use it to the fullest extent that you can.

Record And Replay

I know that some of my clients find it hard to remember all the details of some of the longer steps. Here's a good idea. Try reading the details of each step into any kind of voice recorder, slowly and clearly. Then hit 'Replay' and follow along to the recording.

"A crust eaten in peace is better than a banquet partaken in anxiety."

- Aesop

*Fact File 1:
Understand
Anxiety*

Fact File 1: Understand Anxiety

Relax And Read

To deal with any problem successfully, you first of all have to *understand* it. That's why we're going to start with some useful information. In this chapter and the next, I want to help you understand a few things about anxiety:

- what it is
- what really happens when you experience anxiety
- how you're going to beat it

Once you have this information, I'll guide you through all nine stages of my ACT (Anxiety Clearing Technique) approach.

Let me just mention one point. If you came to see me in real life, I would normally start with ACT 1, which is about making sure you are in a relaxed, confident frame of mind *without* any anxiety. I could have started this book with ACT 1, but I felt it best to give you the 'Fact File' sections first.

So, let me make one thing clear. If you are feeling *any* kind of anxiety or nervousness *right now*, or at any time while reading the next few pages, please turn to ACT 1 on page 42. Then you can come back to this Fact File section. Okay?

You don't *have* to be feeling anxious to use ACT 1. You can go to it at any time, even if you just think you'd like to calm down a bit and get in the right 'mood' to read this first chapter properly.

So, assuming you're feeling relaxed and ready to learn... let's get on with it! The first thing to understand is how feelings arise.

How Feelings Arise

You may never have thought much about how feelings arise. It's the sort of thing that seems rather obvious: nice things make you feel nice, bad things make you feel bad. What could be simpler? In fact, there's a bit more to it than that. In particular, I want to explain this chain of four separate stages:

- Stimulus
- Cognition
- Emotion
- Feeling

As you can see, feelings are just the fourth and final stage. Let me explain how this chain works in a bit more detail.

Stimulus

Every time you experience anxiety, *something* sets it off. The 'something' is the *stimulus*, the trigger that leads to the experience of anxiety. In some cases, you may know what the stimulus is. In other cases, you may *not* know, so you feel as if the anxiety 'just happens'. Nonetheless, there is always a stimulus of some kind. More specifically, it is a stimulus that you have learned to associate with the response of anxiety.

In the main, you perceive the world around you through your senses: sight, hearing, touch, taste and smell. What you perceive through your senses is not reality. It is your *perception* of reality.

In many cases, the stimulus that triggers anxiety comes via your senses and your perception of the world around you. However, in other cases the stimulus may just be a thought. If you imagine something clearly and vividly enough, your mind reacts just as if it were real. To your mind, a real experience and an imaginary one can amount to much the same thing.

So, the chain of events that lead to feelings start with a **Stimulus**. What's next?

Cognition

So, a stimulus gives rise to a perception in your brain. Next, your brain tries to match this new perception to *previous* perceptions, in other words to your memories of previous experiences and how you responded to them. For this reason, you are likely to respond to this *new* stimulus the same way you responded to any *similar* stimulus in the past.

Your brain uses your memories as *reference* material to decide how to respond to the stimulus. Suppose that in the past you have looked at some succulent fruit, tasted it and enjoyed it. Next time you see some fruit that looks just as juicy and tasty; your brain *expects* to enjoy tasting it, based on its reference material from the past.

This process of using stored patterns of stimulus and response is known as 'cognition'. The important point is to realise that you have *learned* all these patterns. They didn't just come from nowhere.

So, we know that Stimulus leads to **Cognition**. What happens next, and where does the anxiety arise?

Emotion

Cognition is the process of associating a stimulus with reference material. Every cognition produces an emotion, based on your past experience.

You can think of an emotion as an electro-chemical 'spark' in your brain. This 'spark' produces profound changes in your body. (This isn't scientifically accurate, but it's good enough for our purposes.)

(There is one exception to this. Your sense of smell initially bypasses the 'cognition' stage and directly stimulates the emotional centres of the brain. This is why smells can be incredibly evocative.)

So a **Stimulus** gives rise to **Cognition** that creates an **Emotion**. Now let's look at the final piece of the jigsaw.

Feeling

You have something called an autonomic nervous system. It is the part of you that takes care of things in your body without you having to think about them. For example, it automatically keeps your heart beating and your lungs breathing, without your conscious control.

When you experience an emotion, it sends a signal to your autonomic nervous system and this creates a *feeling* in your body.

Note that emotions and feelings are not the same thing. You never experience an emotion directly. You can only experience the feeling in your physical body that the emotion has caused. Putting it another way, a feeling is your somatic (bodily) *experience* of an emotion.

As I have said, your autonomic nervous system works outside of your conscious awareness and control. This is why you may sometimes feel that anxiety just happens to you, without any clear or obvious stimulus. In fact, there *is* always a stimulus of some kind, but sometimes you're not aware of it because your reaction to the stimulus is happening at the autonomic level, outside of your awareness.

Feelings are the way you consciously experience changes in your body triggered by emotional reactions.

So there you have the complete chain:

Stimulus > Cognition > Emotion > Feeling

Of course, not all feelings are feelings of anxiety. Sometimes, a particular stimulus can lead to very nice or pleasant feelings. So why does this chain sometimes lead to feelings of anxiety?

How Anxiety Arises

Anxiety is the physical feeling caused by the emotion of fear.

As we have seen, your emotions give rise to your feelings. Nice, happy emotions give rise to nice, happy feelings. However, if the emotion is *fear*, then it can give rise to anxiety.

Every time you feel anxious, the emotion of fear is driving the process. The emotion of fear, via your autonomic nervous system, tells your body to produce hormones such as cortisol and adrenaline which are often referred to as 'stress hormones'. These cause a number of changes in your body.

Your heart beats more quickly. Your breathing increases so you can use more oxygen. This increase in respiration increases the amount of oxygen in your blood. Your heart pumps this highly oxygenated blood around your body, supplying fuel (glucose and oxygen) that your body can convert into energy. Your blood vessels (vascular system) dilate to accommodate this increased blood flow and so your blood pressure increases. You may also find yourself sweating a great deal.

There are several other changes too. Your pupils dilate. You may experience a 'churning' feeling in your stomach. You may have bowel and bladder movements. Your skin may appear pale because the arteries of the skin and intestines become constricted. The muscular activity of the gut is inhibited, and areas of the intestines and bladder constrict because they aren't essential to respond to an urgent threat.

The main feelings you experience with anxiety usually concentrate at a point in your stomach, just below the sternum (chest bone). The organs of the chest and abdominal cavities contain receptors for pain and for detecting the stretching and contraction of muscles. As they move or change, you experience certain feelings as a result.

Minor feelings also come from the skeletal muscles and skin, from receptors that detect pain and the changes in circulation brought on by the autonomic nervous system. You may detect these as tingling, numbness or a sense that you are breaking out into a 'cold sweat'.

These changes in your body are accompanied by a largely automatic change in your body posture. Your skeletal muscles tense and you shift your stance to protect your face, vital organs and sides. This is known as a 'closed' body position.

Panic Attacks

The feelings of anxiety are bad enough, but just to make things worse they can become self-perpetuating.

Whenever the feelings of anxiety are strong enough, you become aware of them. So the feelings themselves become part of your *cognition*. This, in turn, provides more fuel for the emotion of fear. In this way, the anxiety can become like a vicious circle. In extreme cases this can escalate into the experience of an anxiety *attack*.

When someone suffers an anxiety attack, they are often filled with a feeling of impending doom. They may feel as if they are on the verge of something very serious such as a heart attack. They aren't. The body is just reacting to a *perceived* threat as it would if the threat were real. It can be very calming and reassuring to know that this is the case.

Fear Serves A Purpose

Fear does actually serve a *positive* purpose. This can be hard to believe, especially if it is producing anxiety that becomes a serious problem in your life. Nonetheless, it's true. Fear originally evolved to protect you and keep you safe.

Positive emotions move us towards things. Negative emotions move us away. As we have seen, anxiety is driven by fear. Fear is designed to move you away from a threat. In some situations this may protect you from harm or injury.

As you grow and develop, you learn to associate fear with certain experiences. Sometimes you learn to associate fear with things that are genuinely dangerous. However, sometimes the learning process goes a bit wrong and you learn to associate fear with something that is *not* actually dangerous. This is where the problem arises.

A large part of this book is about removing these incorrect associations so you no longer suffer from anxiety.

'Fight Or Flight'

The anxiety response that I have described is often referred to colloquially as the 'fight or flight' response. The usual explanation goes something like this. When a threat is perceived, your brain assesses two possible responses: try to run away from the threat, or stand your ground and try to fight it. Either way, you're going to need all the energy you can get so your body produces adrenaline to increase blood flow to your muscles. As well as 'fight or flight', other names for this process are the 'General Adaptation Syndrome' and the 'Mammalian Stress Response'.

There are actually more stages involved in this response than most people realise. I want to share with you a more detailed and accurate explanation. This will help you to understand so much more about the process, which puts you in a much better position to get rid of anxiety forever.

I call the complete response to a threat the Six F sequence.

The Six F Sequence

When you perceive something as a threat, you go through six response stages. These are the same for everyone. Each stage has developed as part of your natural survival instinct.

First, you look to defuse the situation. This usually means you try to use reasoning or distraction to nullify the threat. This is the main source of the avoidance behaviour typical of many people who suffer from anxiety.

If defusing the threat doesn't work, your stress response increases. You try to stay very still, or 'freeze'. You focus your attention directly on the threat and your body prepares to take whatever action may be necessary. People experiencing a panic attack often freeze and inhale quickly. When you freeze, physical changes take place in your body and these produce feelings of anxiety.

If action is necessary, then you take 'flight' and try to move directly away from the source of the threat.

If this fails, you progress to the next response stage: you 'fight'. This doesn't necessarily entail an actual physical fight. It refers to any direct action you take against the threat, such as an angry outburst or some other display of bad temper.

If the 'fight' response fails to remove the threat, you escalate to 'fear'. You freeze, but this time your attention is directed internally. You feel helpless, unable to take any effective action to deal with threat. This is often the time when trauma becomes encoded in your mind. If the threat continues to intensify, you progress to the sixth and final response stage: you 'faint'.

In summary, the Six F Sequence is:

Anxiety And Behaviour

People who suffer from anxiety tend to exhibit certain behavioural patterns. I'd like to mention four in particular.

Breathing

When you experience anxiety, you often freeze (as described above) but also take a sharp breath in at the same time. This happens for two reasons.

First of all, as we have already seen, your body senses that you need to oxygenate your blood as rapidly as possible.

Secondly, it also happens because you are getting ready to *exhale* if you need to act with urgency. Whenever you physically exert yourself you breathe out. Even just getting up out of a chair, you breathe out as you exert yourself.

In order to breathe out, of course, you first of all need to breathe in. This is why most people breathe in sharply when they have a 'pang' of anxiety, particularly if they have been shocked by something.

I want to reassure you that this sharp breath is a perfectly normal reaction. It doesn't indicate anything seriously wrong. This sharp intake of breath is just a normal bodily response to a perceived threat.

Avoidance

As we have seen, anxiety is a healthy mechanism intended to move you away from some form of threat or danger. However, while moving away from a threat is one good strategy, another is to not let the threat get near in the first place. For this reason, many anxiety sufferers develop behavioural patterns to avoid whatever is perceived as a potential threat. This is known as avoidance behaviour.

If something has made you anxious in the past you may well try to avoid it in the future. For example, if you are anxious about what other people think of you, you may tend to become reclusive and avoid social situations. If you don't like being in the spotlight, you may avoid volunteering to give a presentation at work or, if you couldn't get out of it, decided to be 'ill' on the day to avoid the problem.

Do you ever use avoidance behaviour? It's worth taking a minute to think what anxiety has stopped you from doing.

Displacement

There are lots of little physical signs associated with feelings of anxiety. One of the most obvious is that anxious people move their hands a lot. This is displacement behaviour, although it is also known as pacifying or, in some circles, adapting. The brain knows that the body is under stress, and anxiety is rising. The brain enlists the body to try and provide comfort in both emotional and physical terms. It works to 'displace' the movements that the body wants to create. This also helps to *conceal* anxiety from others — most people don't want anyone else to know they are feeling anxious.

Other common displacement activities include rubbing your neck, stroking your face, playing with your hair, chewing gum, smoking cigarettes, licking your lips, scratching your forearm, pacing up and down, rubbing your earlobe and so on. When you know about these signs, it's fairly easy to spot when people are feeling anxious.

When you know about displacement activity, it can give you an advantage in meetings and negotiations. Displacement behaviour is a very reliable sign that someone is stressed and anxious.

If you ask someone a question and they start to show displacement behaviour, you know you have induced discomfort. You can then apply a little psychological deduction to ascertain the exact cause of their discomfort. By the way, the discomfort and displacement do not *necessarily* mean the person is lying. You *do* know they are feeling discomfort. You do *not* know this discomfort arises from lying — there could be several other reasons.

Group anxiety

Before moving on, it is worth mentioning that anxiety is not confined to individuals. It can spread in an infectious way through a group of friends or work colleagues or any kind of team. In any group, people tend to unconsciously want to follow or mimic whoever is in the strongest state. This is known as 'isopraxism'. For example, if a leader or dominant personality in a group is really happy, the happiness can spread to everyone else. On the other hand, if that person is in a foul mood, it can spread so that fairly soon everyone is irritable and on edge.

It's the same with anxiety. If the person with the strongest state is displaying anxiety, he or she could trigger feelings of anxiety in everyone else who is present.

In this book my focus is on one individual: you. So I won't be spending much time talking about group anxiety. However, after you have read this book and learned how to deal with and eliminate your own anxiety, you will similarly be able to reduce the anxiety of an entire group just by being a strong, relaxed, calm influence on all the others.

Anxiety And Related Issues

The final point I want to make in this section is that anxiety rarely exists as an isolated problem. It is often one element within a wider or more complex issue. The good news is that very often getting rid of the anxiety *also* eliminates the wider issue it is part of. Here are four common examples of the sort of thing I mean. As you read these examples, you may be able to find some correlations with your own life. Think about how anxiety may affect your wider behaviour or be part of a wider problem.

Stress

Stress can be described as fatigue brought on by prolonged anxiety. This fatigue is physical as well as mental. Your body and mind runs 'hot' when suffering from anxiety. If this continues for a period of time your body starts to become run down.

As we have seen, anxiety in the short term serves to help you survive. In the longer term it can cause a breakdown of your body and adversely affect your mind.

We've already learned that during periods of anxiety your body produces the stress hormone cortisol. Your body continues to produce cortisol for as long as the source of the stress is present. If this goes on for a while, the cortisol will promote high blood pressure and high blood sugar. There will be an increase in the storage of body fat, particularly around the stomach, as well as increased facial hair growth, acne, osteoporosis and wasting of skeletal muscles. There is increased risk of hypertension, stroke, diabetes and ulcers. It also leads to suppression of the immune system, which obviously leaves you more susceptible to a whole range of diseases, illnesses and infections.

Cortisol also has adverse effects on your mind. It can lead to problems with thinking and with memory. In extreme cases, it can lead to arousal, hyper-vigilance, delusions, rage and even psychosis.

Clearly, stress leads to many negative consequences for both your mind and your body. When you resolve your anxiety, the symptoms of stress will automatically start to clear up, both physically and mentally.

Depression

Depression can be described as a continued low mood. It is often characterised by certain patterns of behaviour and thought, which work together to sustain and deepen the depression. Anxiety is often one of the symptoms, and also part of the supporting structure.

When you experience anxiety, you are a little bit like a motor or an engine that is 'running hot'. What I mean by this is that your autonomic nervous system is over-reacting. This leaves you more prone to feel anger, which is what you experience when you feel someone has broken your personal rules. You may experience this internally as frustration, or display it externally as an angry outburst of some kind — anything from a mild tantrum to extreme rage.

After you experience or display anger, you probably feel that you have over-reacted or reacted in an inappropriate way. You may feel guilt, or feel shame because you have been seen behaving in this 'bad' way. Other common feelings are regret, remorse and embarrassment. These are all negative emotions about a past event. They often lead to an over-reaction of the autonomic nervous system, which in turn leads to more anxious feelings. It can lead to a vicious cycle and even panic attacks.

When you resolve anxiety, you usually achieve greater acceptance of yourself and whatever has happened, which leads to reduced anger. Hence you reduce the negative emotions about a past event. By following the ACT system and resolving anxiety, the supporting structure for depression, and indeed many anger issues, automatically collapses.

Insomnia

My clients with difficulties getting to sleep often tell me that their insomnia causes them to be anxious throughout the day. In my experience, it's often the other way around. I have found that in the case of clients who find it hard to go to sleep, or who wake early and can't sleep again, anxiety is the *cause* of the problem rather than a *symptom* of it. When I help these clients resolve the anxiety, the insomnia usually clears up as well. If you have trouble sleeping, especially with the patterns above, when you follow the ACT system your sleep issues should be a thing of the past.

Trauma

Traumatic events often leave people with deep seated anxiety, especially when faced with things that remind them of the trauma. They sense the stimulus, draw the correlation in their mind with the trauma, experience the emotion of fear, and feel the anxiety.

In this book, one of the things I will show you how to do is reduce or eliminate the fear element that is associated (in your memory) with the original traumatic event.

Applying The Knowledge

In this section, we have taken quite a bit of time to understand what anxiety really is, and to study all the processes that your body goes through when you experience anxiety.

This knowledge can be helpful in any situation where anxiety arises. For example, we looked at how anxiety affects breathing. You can stop yourself feeling more anxious just by saying to yourself, "Oh, that's just my breathing increasing due to a perceived threat — it's a perfectly normal, natural response and nothing to be scared of. I just need to realise that in *this* case the threat isn't real, and I'm not *actually* going to come to any harm."

I've already mentioned another example: when someone suffers a lot of anxiety they often feel as if they are on the verge of something very serious such as a heart attack. It can be very reassuring to know that this is not the case. If you're suffering this kind of panic attack, you can say to yourself, "I'm not having a heart attack. My body is just reacting naturally to a perceived threat and doing exactly what it would do *if* the threat were real. But it isn't real, and I'm going to be okay."

Summary

- Understanding anxiety is the key to getting rid of it forever.
- A stimulus passes through cognition and is perceived as a threat. This creates the emotion of fear. The fear causes changes in the body that create the feeling of anxiety.
- This feeling can feed back into your cognition, creating a vicious circle.
- Anxiety serves a positive purpose. It is to keep you safe from threats.
- Anxiety leads to specific behaviours such as breathing patterns, avoidance and displacement behaviour. Anxiety can also spread through groups of people like a virus.
- Anxiety often sits within wider issues, such as stress, depression, insomnia and trauma. When you remove the anxiety, you will often solve the wider issue as well.

This was the first of two 'Fact File' chapters. The aim of these two chapters is to help you understand the nature of anxiety better than ever before, so that you will be well-equipped to tackle the problem and overcome it.

The next chapter is another 'Fact File' chapter, but I think you'll find it interesting — particularly since I'll be explaining how to reach a point where you can get rid of anxiety *almost* as if by magic!

"I've developed a new philosophy... I only dread one day at a time."

– Charles Schulz

Fact File 2: Understand Your Mind

Fact File 2: Understand Your Mind

Learning To Change

As I said at the start of the first Fact File chapter, you can deal with any problem successfully provided you first of all *understand* it.

The first Fact File chapter was mainly about understanding the nature of anxiety itself.

This second Fact File chapter is mainly about understanding your mind, or at least some important aspects of how the mind works and how behavioural patterns are formed. You will learn how to bring about some very positive changes in your mind and in yourself.

This chapter gets a bit technical in parts. If you find it hard going at first, just skim over the paragraphs until you get to the summary. However, if you take the time to read this section carefully, you'll learn plenty of useful information.

Before we get started, take a moment to consider this question: if you could learn to change *any* aspect of the way you currently think, act and behave, what would you change?

Stimulus And Response

Whether you realise it or not, you *learned* to be anxious. The good news is that just as you learned to be anxious, you can learn *not* to be anxious ever again.

You are learning from the moment you are born. Your brain is continuously making new connections and forming new patterns of stimulus and response. You see ice-cream for the first time, eat some, and discover you enjoy the sweet, creamy taste. Next time you experience the same stimulus (seeing ice-cream) you are inclined to repeat the response (eat it). The more often you do this, the more likely you are to repeat the same behaviour in future.

31

Let's consider a different example. You are very young and you see a naked flame. It looks pretty. You reach out to touch it and experience some pain because it's too hot. You learn to avoid getting too near to a flame. Next time you experience the same stimulus (seeing or feeling the heat from a naked flame) you are inclined to repeat the same response (withdraw and keep yourself a safe distance away). Just to repeat the point: the more often you do this, the more likely you are to repeat the same behaviour in future.

The study of the nervous system is called neurology. A fundamental principle of neurology is commonly expressed as 'what fires together wires together'. This means that the patterns we've been looking at, where a given stimulus becomes associated with a given response, become 'wired in' to your brain. This is how you learn to associate a stimulus with a response (the process is often referred to as 'associated learning'). We know that repetition and emotional intensity both assist the process. Both can help to make the 'wiring together' happen more quickly, or more securely.

Each specific pattern of stimulus and response is known as a *behaviour*. Patterns that you use often (behaviours that you repeat regularly) become stronger and re-enforced over time. Patterns that you seldom use (behaviours that you rarely if ever repeat) gradually weaken over time and may eventually deteriorate so the pattern no longer exists in your mind. It's like the familiar saying, 'use it or lose it'!

These patterns of behaviour (stimulus and response) in your brain form your memories. These become your mind's reference material. They guide how you respond to any particular stimulus.

So why do you sometimes experience anxiety? Because you have learned to associate this response (feeling anxious) with one or more stimuli. The good news is that you can break this pattern and replace it with a different one, such as experiencing exactly the same stimulus but responding with calm, relaxed feelings. A large part of this book is about teaching you exactly how to do this!

Perception And Reality

In the previous chapter I explained that what you tend to think of as 'reality' is really nothing of the kind. It's just your *perception* of reality, formed in your mind from sensory information. Although we have already touched on this point, in this chapter I want to go into a little more detail.

Consider your sense of sight.

Light reflects off objects and is detected by cells at the back of your eye, on the retina, that are known as rods and cones. You have around 60 million of these in either eye. These cells send an electro-chemical signal to your visual cortex, where it is analysed for movement, colour, contrast, distance and other factors.

Your brain cross-references this signal against previous perceptions stored in your memory. It does not do this with perfect accuracy! Your brain is prone to deleting, distorting and generalising information (don't feel insulted — this is true for you, me and everyone else). Your brain looks for what is 'familiar' and tries to fit what you see into a pattern it already knows. Only then, after all of this processing and filtering, is the 'image' formed inside your mind.

In short, the image inside your mind is just a perception of reality, affected by your previous experiences. Of course, all of this happens almost instantly, and without you being aware of it.

Here's a good example of the difference between perception and reality. In each of your eyes you have what is referred to as a 'blind' spot, which is where the optic nerve joins the retina at the back of your eye. There are no rods and cones at this location, and therefore this part of your retina doesn't send any signal.

However, when you look at something, you don't see a part of the scene 'missing' because of these blind spots. Why not? Because your mind fills in the gaps. It uses whatever information it has about the scene to imagine the missing part and create the perception of a complete image.

Everyone's path in life is different, so everyone learns different patterns and perceptions. We've all seen two people arguing about an experience like this:

> *"Then it happened like this."*
> *"No it didn't, it happened like this!"*
> *"Look, I was there, I know how it happened, and I'm right!"*
> *"I was there too! You're wrong, I'm right!"*

One or both of these people may be wrong about the reality of what they *saw*. However, they are both right in terms of what they *perceived*.

Everyone perceives reality differently. If we could all understand and respect this simple truth, there would be many fewer arguments in the world. Particularly in the pub.

This doesn't just apply to what you see. The same is true for all of your senses. Every perception you have is affected by your past experiences.

What has this got to do with anxiety? Well, people with anxiety tend to filter their perception to notice whatever is bad or worrying *more* than they notice whatever is good or positive. They see the worst rather than the best. They are also prone to hallucinate and to read more into situations than is really there. Their internal self-talk, their speech and their physiology will all reflect their skewed perception. We will return to this point later.

In summary, *you do not see reality*. You see a *version* of reality, your perception, which is distorted by your *memories* based on past experience. The good news is that your memories are not permanent, fixed and unchangeable. Quite the opposite.

Memories Are Plastic

Memories are plastic, by which I mean they can be modified, deformed and distorted. When you recall something, that memory becomes modified by your current emotional and physical state. It is the modified (and perhaps even distorted) version of that memory that gets stored for later retrieval. Think of it like a document stored on a computer: you open the file, make some changes and save it again.

As we have already seen, your memories are your reference material. They affect your current perceptions. Since your memories can become changed and distorted, your reference material changes and so does your perception.

The bad news is that we very often don't realise this has happened, and a distorted memory can lead to a perception that leads to anxiety. The *good* news is that you can consciously and purposefully change your memories in a *positive* way, so that you behave and act differently. This is a large part of learning to overcome anxiety forever.

Types Of Memories

Not all memories are the same. Your memories fall into five different categories: genetic, emotional, episodic, procedural and semantic.

As the name implies, your genetic memories arise from your genes. Your genes determine many aspects of your physical body and, some experts would say, of your mind as well. Your genetic memories include all your autonomic survival responses, including the stress response. Although this exists for a good reason, it can give rise to feelings of anxiety in your body.

Emotional memories are ones that attach an emotion to a stimulus. If a stimulus gives rise to anxiety, it means you have learnt to attach the emotion of fear to that stimulus. The attachment is based on an emotional memory.

Episodic memories are little stories or narratives from your life. They have a start, middle and end, and are stored in your memory almost like a short movie. Episodic memories tend to be primarily visual though they may include other sensations too, such as sounds, tastes and smells. Episodic memories provide a context in which an emotion is experienced.

Procedural memories take care of all the actions or behaviours that you can carry out automatically or habitually, virtually without thinking. Examples would include driving, riding a bike or tying a shoelace. The important point to note is that procedural memories involve little or no conscious thought. If you sometimes feel anxiety 'just happens' for no real reason, it's probably because a procedural memory is involved: one that includes recalling either anxious feelings from the past or events that can trigger your anxiety response.

Semantic memories are your knowledge base. They cover all the facts, figures and information that you have learned. Semantic memories can create anxiety through learned expectations and behaviour learned from others.

A Learned Fear

Some experts suggest we are born with only two innate, natural fears: falling and loud noises. If you are afraid or fearful of anything else, you must have learned that fear at some point in your life.

Earlier, we looked at a simple model of 'stimulus and response'. When you are presented with a given stimulus you will use the reference material from your memories to develop a pattern of behaviour in response to that stimulus. This pattern is known as a strategy or (in more formal terms) a 'schema'. If you suffer from anxiety, it means you have a schema that includes experiencing anxiety.

In simple terms, at some point in your life you learned a schema that includes responding in an anxious way to this or that stimulus. The good news is that you can learn a different schema.

I'd like to mention one particularly striking example of just how quickly your mind can learn a new pattern (which is not always a good thing), and how far reaching these changes can be.

As a therapist, I sometimes work with military personnel suffering from PTSD (Post-Traumatic Stress Disorder). PTSD is a perfect example of how, in an instant, the mind can make deep changes that can affect someone's thought, action and behaviour. It truly is remarkable how quickly this can happen. A split second may be all it takes.

When someone experiences a deeply traumatic event, it can give rise to an intensely negative emotion. If their perception, at the time, is that there is simply no way to escape from the traumatic event, this can have an intense, devastating and enduring effect. The PTSD becomes encoded in a second, with very harmful effects on the individual's mind and behaviour.

People suffering from PTSD suffer from a host of symptoms, such as anger, anxiety, guilt and low self-esteem. They find that almost any stimulus can set off adverse reactions, such as flashbacks, and over time this will only get worse: more and more different stimuli will tend to trigger these symptoms. The person's body may 'remember' the trauma, leading to numerous physical ailments and problems. It's as if the patient becomes stuck in the trauma.

The study of PTSD shows us that negative changes to the mind's repertoire of responses can occur in an instant. The good news is that if we find the right key, and the right emotion, we can just as quickly bring about a *positive* change. By giving the patient the right mental training, we can help him or her to overcome the PTSD and leave the past behind.

In the same way, if you study how you learned to develop anxiety, and the strategy or schema you use to sustain it, you can very rapidly create changes that end the anxiety issues once and for all.

Un-learning anxiety

So how can you learn to be free from anxiety?

There are two parts to the solution.

First of all, you can learn to *control* anxiety. You can learn *not* to react to the stimulus in an anxious way. It's like flicking a switch from the 'on' position to 'off'.

Secondly, you can learn to *regulate* anxiety. You can learn to experience just the right amount of anxiety that is appropriate for the stimulus. This is like turning a dial to regulate just how strong the anxiety is, while keeping it under control at all times.

Bear both of these images in mind as you progress through this book: the switch and the dial.

Sometimes you will be learning to use mental switches that turn certain feelings and responses on or off.

Sometimes you will be learning to use mental dials that allow you to increase or decrease a feeling or a response, as you wish.

Summary

- Anxiety is a learned behaviour. You only feel anxious because you have learned to do so. The anxiety reaction has become encoded in your neurology through past experience.

- You do not experience reality directly. You experience your perception of reality, which is affected by your past experiences.

- Your past experience gives you your memories which guide you how to act in the present. They become your reference material. Memories are plastic, so you can change this reference material and learn a different way to respond.

- You can learn to control and regulate anxiety through simple 'interventions' that help you to create new connections in your mind.

In this second Fact File chapter, you gained a better understanding of your mind, memories and behaviours, and discovered how it's possible to change some aspects of your mind to solve your anxiety problem forever.

With all this preparatory work completed, you can now begin the change process. It is time for you to become completely and utterly free from anxiety, forever!

There are nine stages in what I call my Anxiety Clearing Technique (ACT). Not surprisingly, your journey starts with ACT 1...

Act 1
Calm Your Mind

ACT 1: Calm your mind

Starting To Change

Every time a new client comes to see me I ask the same question:

"So, what are we here for today?"

Surprisingly, many of my clients find this question rather hard to answer. They find it difficult to put the exact reason for coming to see me into words. Some of them even end up asking *me* why they have come to see me!

This is understandable, and I sympathise with each and every person that comes to see me. People suffering from anxiety have minds that are racing. They tend to have what I playfully refer to as the 'chattering monkeys' going on inside their mind all the time — those voices of doubt, stress and anxiety that are constantly jabbering away and suggesting things to worry about. All in all, many of my clients are neither relaxed nor focused enough to express themselves clearly or listen to me properly.

The same will be true for most of you reading this book. How much noise is going on inside your mind?

For us to work together successfully, my first job is to help you to calm down so that you can focus, pay attention and develop the skills you will need to overcome anxiety forever.

To calm you down now, and give you a little space from anxiety, let me share with you Steps 1 and 2 of the ACT approach. Each of these steps on their own will lower your anxiety immediately, and each is presented here for a specific reason. Please follow both through carefully, and allow your mind to calm down.

Here's step 1 of the ACT approach.

Step 1: The Mind Game

You will need something small and light that you can throw from hand to hand. It can be a tennis ball, a squash ball or something similar. You can even use a small potato or a piece of paper rolled into a ball.

Here's what to do. Remember to read this over several times. You want to understand what you are going to do before you actually do it.

- Notice how you feel inside. Focus on what your anxiety is like right now, and rate it on a scale from 1 to 10, where 10 is the maximum. Be precise.
- Take the ball and throw it from hand to hand, across your body, with rhythm (1, 2, 1, 2, 1, 2). The hand doing the throwing makes most of the movement. The hand receiving the ball moves very little.
- When you can throw the ball continuously, look up through your eyebrows, keeping your head facing forward.
- Continue for 30 seconds then stop.
- Check how you feel inside now. Rate your anxiety on a scale from 1 to 10.
- Repeat this step until your anxiety is down to 3 or below.

(Did this work for you? This is a simple yet highly effective technique. Just about everyone who tries this finds that it is a very good way to quickly lower anxiety. If it didn't seem to work for you, try it again yet exaggerate the movements across the body and try to find and maintain a rhythm.)

Now let's take it further:

- Try to get your anxiety up as high as you possibly can.
- Once you have it as high as you can, repeat the ball throwing and looking up until your anxiety is back down to a 3 or less.
- Try to raise your anxiety again, and repeat the whole process.
- Continue repeating until you can't get any anxiety back, or you run out of time you have available.

How did it go?

You will notice that I have called Step 1 'The Mind Game'. This is a reasonably accurate description of what's going on. You are distracting your mind by giving it something else to think about — a simple game that involves physical movement and rhythm, and that requires a small amount of concentration. This also has the effect of quietening or silencing what I refer to as the 'chattering monkeys' or negative internal dialogue that plagues so many people who suffer from anxiety.

I'll talk more about why this works so well later. For now, I am just using it to achieve a simple purpose. It lowers your anxiety and calms you down to the point where you can focus on the information I am sharing with you.

'The Mind Game' also helps you to relax physically. Your breathing becomes easier and your whole body becomes calmer. Don't resist this! *Allow* your body to adopt a more relaxed posture.

I suggest you repeat this simple step whenever you feel you are too anxious to read this book properly or feel you just aren't taking anything in. You'll create a neurological distraction that has the effect of lowering your level of anxiety. You then create the anxiety again and lower it, repeatedly.

Many people say that anxiety just happens to them. When you use this step, you *create* anxiety and you *take it away*. You are *in control*.

When you begin to feel that you're in control, because you can create and remove anxiety at will, you may well start to wonder when you will simply stop feeling anxious in the first place!

Just in case Step 1 didn't work for you as well as it can, and also to give you an alternative step to use, let's move straight on to Step 2 of the ACT approach. Even if Step 1 worked well, please still do Step 2 as well. I want you to learn all the steps, and all the skills, that will help you to get rid of anxiety issues forever.

(Step 2 is on the next page.)

Step 2: Playing With Feelings

Can you get any feelings of anxiety back now?

Earlier in this book I explained exactly what anxious feelings are, how they are created and sustained, and the physical effects they cause in your body. In Step 2, we use this knowledge to release anxiety and let it go.

To allow your anxiety to go, you first of all need to be feeling some anxiety! It may be difficult to feel anxious after carrying out Step 1, but try imagining a situation in which you would experience the normal anxiety symptoms, such as a churning feeling ('butterflies') in your stomach, an accelerated heart rate and rapid, shallow breathing. As you think about one or more situations that make you anxious, you should be able to allow those feelings to come to you now.

As we have already seen, you experience these feelings of anxiety in your body. If you mentally focus on these feelings, and ask yourself *where* you feel them, you will find they do seem to have a physical location inside of you. Pay attention to your anxiety and note where this feeling is in your body. Most people say it's like a churning feeling in the stomach at a point in the upper abdomen just below the sternum.

Next, I want you to notice how it can appear to move, maybe turning one way, or moving another way. Also, notice its size (and maybe its shape). I'd like you to really pay attention to the way that your anxiety feels in your body.

Paying close attention to your anxiety and exactly how it feels to you is an important step towards understanding it and dealing with it effectively. At this stage, I want you to concentrate on the *physical* aspects of anxiety and learn how to manage the *experience* of anxiety effectively.

When you carry out Step 2, provided you follow all the instructions closely, you will experience something that feels almost magical: you will learn a simple way to control your body with your mind. As a result, you will learn how to reduce, and potentially remove, any feelings of anxiety.

As with Step 1, please read this over several times. You want to *understand* what you are going to do *before* you actually do it. Here's what to do.

- Close your eyes and focus on the feeling in your body
- Note how intense the feeling is on a scale from 1 to 10
- If this feeling had a colour, what colour would it be?
- Change the colour to something you find more soothing and relaxing, such as a warming yellow or a cooling blue. Choose whatever works for you.
- Notice the way that the feeling is moving. You'll probably find the feeling seems to 'spin' or turn in a certain direction. Wait until you have a distinct sense of whatever the sensation of movement is.
- Whatever the sensation of movement is, slow it down by half.
- Slow the feeling down by half again.
- Slow the feeling down until it comes to a complete stop, and then set it going in the *opposite* direction.
- Notice the physical size of the feeling. Does it seem large or small?
- Shrink it by half.
- Shrink it by half again.
- Shrink it down to the size of a pea.
- Take that pea and 'pop' it outside of your body so that it is in front of you.
- Fire that pea off into the distance, so it sinks to the bottom of the deepest ocean or burns up in the sun.
- Open your eyes for a moment.
- Close your eyes. Notice how strong the feeling is now on a scale of 1 to 10.

(Did Step 2 work for you? How did it go? Couldn't get a colour? Just imagine what colour it would have if it had one. Couldn't detect the movement? Remove distractions, go somewhere quiet, and really become mindful of the feeling in your body. Couldn't slow the movement, or couldn't shrink it down? Use your imagination. Your body will create whatever you imagine. Just imagine the movement slowing, imagine the feeling getting smaller, imagine 'popping' it out of your body.)

If you don't completely succeed with Step 2 at first, don't worry — nothing bad will happen! However, most of you will experience significant change.

Step 2 works because you use your imagination to guide your body to make changes. It is a *metaphorical* way of working that gets the results.

Step 2 doesn't just work on the feelings of anxiety. If you have *any* sort of feeling that you want to get rid of, you can use step 2 to get rid of it. For example, I regularly use Step 2 for a quick bit of pain relief without needing to take a painkiller. Pain is real, yet pain is also a perception in the emotional centre of your brain. As such you can use Step 2 to help you change your perception of whatever pain you may be dealing with.

Let me just clarify that last point. Pain serves a useful function. It is your body's way of telling you to pay attention to a problem. If you ignore the signal for too long, the problem will just get worse. For this reason, I am not suggesting you use Step 2 to *ignore* pain. I'm just saying it can be a handy little intervention when you have a headache, or minor sports injury, and you need some quick relief until you can address the problem in a more comprehensive way.

You now have two steps that you can use in order to reduce and remove anxiety. Practise them as much as you possibly can.

The Magic Of Imagination

Procedural Memory

Suppose I told you I could give you a way of eliminating anxiety that worked *almost* like magic! You'd be very interested, wouldn't you? Well, I can do this, or at least get pretty close to it, but first I need to explain a couple of ideas.

The first is the notion of a procedural memory.

The second is the power of imagined reality.

I'll start with the concept of a procedural memory. We have already seen that whenever you repeatedly perform a task, in your mind or with your body, it becomes 'wired in' to your neurology. In other words, you form a habit. The more often you perform the same task, the easier it becomes for you and the more efficiently you can carry it out.

When you take this process to a certain level, you create what is called a *procedural* memory. Simple examples of procedural memories would be driving, typing, tying your shoelaces or riding a bike. If you have learned to do any of these things, you have probably reached the stage where you can do them easily, instantly and effortlessly.

Note those characteristics: easily, instantly and effortlessly. These are the typical characteristics of anything that you have learned and stored as a procedural memory.

Here's the point: I'd like you to practise Steps 1 and 2 as often as you possibly can so that you build a procedural memory for both. Each and every time you carry out these steps you are building a procedural memory. In fact, you are building a *habit of removing anxiety*.

So, practise Steps 1 and 2 until you can do them both easily, instantly and effortlessly, like tying a shoelace or riding a bike.

Good! We're nearly getting to the 'magic' part!

Now let me explain what I mean by imagined reality.

Imagined Reality

If you *vividly* imagine something, your mind and body react just as if it were real. Putting it another way, your mind and body respond to an *imagined* stimulus exactly as they would respond to a real one.

Try this little mental exercise. Imagine cutting into a nice, fresh juicy lemon. See the colours, make them bright and bold. Imagine cutting the lemon into pieces. Imagine the juices that flow from the flesh of the lemon. Imagine the lemon fragrance, and imagine what the lemon feels like in your hands. Now take a piece of that imaginary lemon and squeeze the juice into your mouth. Imagine that sharp, tangy, citrus taste, and the lemon fragrance filling your nose. Imagine all the sensations of that lemon as you see it, touch it, smell it and taste it.

When you try this, you may find you start to salivate in exactly the same way you would if you were *actually* eating a slice of lemon. This is a simple example of the power of your imagination. The more vividly you can imagine something, the more closely your mind and body will respond *as if the experience were real*.

So, here's the 'magic' that I promised. You know Steps 1 and 2, that you have already learned? You can perform those steps *in your imagination*, and get exactly the same benefit as if you were actually performing them for real!

Now, let me quickly qualify this statement so you don't get the wrong idea. First of all, this will only work if you have developed the *procedural memories* that I have already explained. You have to have practised Step 1 and Step 2 so often that you have built up strong procedural memories.

Secondly, your imagination has to be good and *vivid*. There will be many times in this book when I ask you to imagine something. The more successfully you can imagine it, the more real it will become for you. When you imagine something, involve all of your senses (just like you did with the 'cutting into a lemon' exercise). Also, try to imagine as many small details as possible.

Each time I ask you to imagine something, imagine it to the very best of your ability and try to make it real. See what you would see, hear what you would hear, and experience what you would experience. Like everything else in life, this gets easier and better with practice. The more often you try using your imagination, the better you will become at imagining different feelings, situations and experiences.

Provided you have built up procedural memories, and practised the power of your imagination, then the 'magic' will work: you can perform Steps 1 and 2 in your imagination and get the same benefit as you would if you did them for real! Your mind and body will respond exactly as if you were actually performing both steps. Isn't that amazing?

It's very useful to progress from actually performing the steps in this book to being able to perform them in your imagination. Why? Because anxiety can arise at any time, even when it's very inconvenient. You may find yourself feeling anxious in a situation where it's not practical to close your eyes or start juggling a ball from hand to hand. However, you can always perform these steps in your mind, inside the privacy of your imagination.

But wait a minute… the magic isn't over yet!

We can take this still further. How about just completely imagining away your anxiety? This may sound a bit too simple, but I promise you it's possible. Think of it as a series of stages in your ability to control and overcome anxiety.

The first stage is to learn the steps that I teach you in this book, and actually perform them in reality.

The second stage is to practise the steps so often that you build up procedural memories (so you can perform them easily, instantly and effortlessly).

The third stage is to cultivate the power of vivid imagination, so that you can perform these steps in the quiet and privacy of your own mind. Your mind and body will respond in the same way as if you were performing the steps for real.

The fourth stage is just to imagine that you have performed the third stage! That's right… instead of actually imagining Step 1 or whatever it is, you simply imagine having already done this! You can imagine reaching the same end result of feeling calm and at ease.

I know this sounds a bit complex (imagining having imagined something). However, I promise you if you read it over a few times and see how each stage builds on the one before, you'll see it does actually make sense!

Of course it takes time, effort and patience to get to this stage. You won't get there overnight or next week. But you *can* get there.

This means that whenever you notice some anxiety, you will be able to use the power of your imagination to overcome it. You will be able to just imagine yourself feeling completely calm and at ease. You will imagine this happening so automatically that there's nothing you can do about it — you immediately become calm and at ease.

When you get to this stage, you may also use the metaphor or mental image of a dial that you can use to take your level of anxiety up or down. As soon as you notice anxiety, think of the dial and imagine how high it is turned up. Then imagine turning the dial down, so that the anxiety turns down too. Your mind and your body know what the dial represents, and will respond accordingly.

Summary

In this section you have taken the first steps towards controlling your anxiety. You have learned that you can create anxiety and also get rid of it.

- Step 1, 'The Mind Game', and Step 2, 'Playing with feelings', help you to regulate and control anxiety. By repeatedly building up anxiety and taking it away again, you are learning to bring it under your control.

- The more times you practise removing your anxiety using Step 1 and Step 2 the more of a habit, a 'procedural memory', you will build.

- Procedural memories, plus the power of imagined reality, mean that you can (with practice) simply 'imagine' your anxiety away.

Congratulations!

In ACT 1, you completed these steps:

Step 1: 'The Mind Game'

Step 2: 'Playing With Feelings'

You are well on the way to living your life free from anxiety or worry forever. ACT 2 will build on this work and give you some additional tools for reducing and eliminating anxiety forever.

"The components of anxiety, stress, fear, and anger do not exist independently of you in the world. They simply do not exist in the physical world, even though we talk about them as if they do."

- Wayne Dyer

*Act 2
Distract
Your Mind*

ACT 2: Distract Your Mind

ACT 1 was principally about dealing with the *symptoms* of anxiety. (We'll start working on the causes very soon.)

In ACT 2, I want to give you some more ways to lower your anxiety immediately. I will put you back in control, so that you can regulate how much anxiety you feel at any time. I will also show you ways to lower your anxiety without consciously doing anything, and do the same for others.

If ever you feel anxious while you progress through this book, just repeat the steps in ACT 1 and allow yourself to feel calm once more.

The Four-legged Therapist

My clients often arrive for hypnotherapy sessions too anxious for me to work with them. They need to calm down so they can listen to me, concentrate and get the full benefit from the session. I have already shared two examples of how I do this in Step 1 and Step 2.

When I want to help my clients to calm down, I have a secret weapon: Max, my youngest husky!

Max was a re-homed husky I took in at 10 months old. Because he used to have separation anxiety, I couldn't leave him on his own while I was conducting my hypnotherapy sessions. I therefore allowed him to come with me, and he used to sit quietly at my client's feet. I gradually realised I had inadvertently trained a brilliant therapy dog!

Dogs can smell chemical changes associated with different emotions. I noticed that Max was detecting my client's emotional state and modifying his behaviour accordingly, such as sitting in a different position or adopting a different posture. I soon began using Max to help me spot subtle indications of anxiety.

I also use Max to *reduce* a client's anxiety. I firmly believe it is impossible to feel anxious while snuggling a husky. Huskies are always friendly towards people. Even clients who say they are afraid of dogs aren't afraid of my huskies. So I get my anxious clients to snuggle Max. I watch their physiology and facial micro-expressions, and it's soon clear that their anxiety is significantly decreased.

Why does this work? Because snuggling Max produces a complete neurological distraction that is *incompatible with feeling anxious*. Let's look at this in a bit more detail, because it will illustrate another excellent way to reduce your anxiety.

Using Distraction

Your brain is divided into left and right hemispheres. These are connected by a sort of 'information superhighway' known as the corpus callosum. The left hemisphere of the brain controls the right side of the body, and vice versa.

Broadly speaking, the left hemisphere is the analytical side of your brain. It handles logic, speech and language, and focuses on specific details rather than the larger picture. The right hemisphere is the creative and imaginative side of your brain. It focuses on the overall picture and provides the 'holistic' view of any given subject. (These are broad generalisations.)

Brain scans show that anxiety is associated with over-activity in the left hemisphere and under-activity in the right hemisphere. As the left hemisphere is responsible for speech, including your internal voice, it follows that when you feel anxious the 'chattering monkeys' are working overtime!

When a client snuggles Max, they of course use both hands. Relatively large areas of the brain are dedicated to receiving signals from the hands, so the snuggling stimulates both hemispheres of the brain to a significant degree. This reduces anxiety because the right hemisphere is now more active.

Anxious people tend to use their hands a lot in a restless, fidgeting manner. This is a *pattern* associated with anxiety. By getting them to do something different with their hands, I help them to *break* this pattern. This is why I get them to stroke and interact with Max, my soft fluffy fur-baby!

Cuddling and interacting with a husky is a source of pleasure. You cannot feel a positive emotion if a negative emotion is present — it is a neurological impossibility. So the constant interaction with Max simply doesn't allow the negative emotion (fear) to persist or to develop.

Anxious people adopt a certain posture where they are tense and can 'close off' their body. When they stroke Max they are forced to let go of the anxiety posture and adopt a relaxed, open, non-anxious posture instead.

When my client interacts with Max, they of course start to talk to him. I encourage this, because it means they are utilising the two areas responsible for self-talk in a different way. The negative self-talk is pushed to one side as they talk in a generally soft and friendly manner with Max. There is only so much you can do at once.

There's one last little trick I use. Max isn't allowed on chairs so my client has to bend forward to greet him and start playing with him. While this is happening, I talk to my client and get him to look up at me from their sitting position. People suffering from anxiety usually look down and to one side, as this helps them neurologically access their self-talk (they may also be feeling introverted). My clients can't do this while they are playing with Max and talking to me, as they need to look up. This makes it harder for them to access self-talk. It also engages a part of the brain known as the temporal lobes, which are not usually associated with anxiety.

In all these various ways, snuggling Max provides my client with a nice neurological distraction from anxiety. In fact, my client is experiencing a range of sensations that are *incompatible with anxiety*. They soon find that they don't feel anxious any more, and instead feel relaxed, calm and happy.

Snuggling a husky reduces anxiety by providing neurological distraction. The same is true of the Step 1 in this book, 'The Mind Game'. You are using both sides of your brain and occupying your hands while looking up. I have just illustrated a different way I use this principle. Perhaps you can start to think of other ways that you can physically create a neurological distraction?

Step 3: Body And Mind

Most people who feel anxious tend to use their body in a certain way. They look down, withdraw in a protective way, tense up and fidget . They adopt a posture that helps them to access anxious feelings (as explained in 'Fact File Part 1').

To remove anxiety, you need to look up, open up your body so you are no longer defensive, relax, use your hands differently and with control, and turn the self-talk around so that it actually starts working in a positive way. By doing things differently, you get a different result. By doing things that are incompatible with anxiety, you will no longer be *able* to feel anxious.

The changes you make do not have to be massive. Quite small adjustments in your body position and the way you move can lead to significant changes in your mood. This next step will prove this. Don't do this publicly... just do it privately, at home, where no-one can see you!

- Think of something that gives you a negative feeling
- Allow your body to move into whatever position and posture helps you to access the negative feeling, and try to make the feeling as intense as you can
- Notice how you feel
- Now stand up (if you haven't already), open your arms, spread your legs wide, lift your head up, open your eyes and allow a smile onto your face
- Now notice how you feel

(Did this work for you? Couldn't get your body to change that negative posture? Become mindful of what your body wants to do. Notice your hands, feet, head and posture. It's hard to consciously access an unconscious reaction, so just go with the flow!

Didn't feel different when you stood up? Give it a little time. Some clients experience changes happening quite quickly, whereas others can take up to two minutes to achieve the intended changes.)

You should notice that you feel *very* different. You should find that you simply cannot hold onto the original feeling. It will either decrease in intensity or disappear altogether.

This is a very powerful principle: change what you do, and you change what you experience. Change what is associated with anxiety, and the anxiety is diminished.

Learn to adopt a different posture than the one you use to access anxiety. Use your body in different ways, so you no longer move the way you do when experiencing (or accessing) anxiety.

You can extend this idea to many areas of your life. Make little changes in your home and your workplace. Change your routine, do things differently. Go to work earlier or later. Take a different route. Walk or cycle whenever possible (exercise also stimulates the release of 'feel good' hormones, and you'll be getting fitter — a double benefit!).

Do things that you've always wanted to do. Take up a new sport or activity, develop a new interest or hobby, or take the time to see some friends. All in all, do as much as you can to change the patterns in your life that are associated with anxiety.

Step 4: Music Magic

If you suffer from anxiety, there will be certain experiences that you associate with a negative emotion. However, there will be other memories that you associate with feeling *great*. All you need to do is access them.

A good way to do this is think of a piece of music that puts you in a great mood. Take your time, imagine listening to that particular music, and allow that happy, positive feeling to flow through you. Of course you don't have to just imagine it... if you can actually listen to the music, do so!

You have associated a piece of music with a good feeling. You can now use that music to lower anxiety or even get rid of it entirely. Remember that you need your body in a certain position and to move it a certain way to experience anxiety? Each and every time you have a negative emotion you will tense up and start to close off. Positive emotions make you open up and relax. Each time you hear that piece of music you are feeling positive, physically opening up and relaxing. Hold on to that feeling by listening to the music as you think of whatever made you anxious. You will imprint the new positive emotion on it and collapse the anxiety away.

- Close your eyes.
- Think of whatever makes you anxious.
- Think of the music that gives you a good feeling.
- Imagine listening to that piece of music and play it loudly in your mind.
- Let it play for a short while.
- As it plays, notice how you now feel.

(Did this work for you? Didn't work? Then find a different piece of music, one that you associate with really powerful, good feelings. It may just be a great piece of music, or one that you associate with happy memories.)

If the association between the music and the good feeling is strong enough, you may find it hard to access any anxiety at all when you use this step. If so, your emotional attachment to the music is greater than the anxiety, enabling you to completely 'collapse' the old anxiety reaction.

Remember that the brain is plastic, as are your memories. Every time you access your memories you change them. You are breaking old connections in your brain and making fresh ones. You are overwriting memories and giving yourself new reference material.

You can use this step on anything negative from the past. Before you do, ensure that you have built up a great feeling inside, and only then access the old negative experience.

You don't need to do this with music, which obviously works via your sense of hearing. You can also use smells. Your sense of smell bypasses cognition and goes straight to the emotional centre of the brain. This is one of the many reasons aromatherapy works so well. Aromatherapists utilise the smells of the aromatic oils to generate the associations they want — which often includes lavender to help bring calm.

To use a smell instead of a piece of music find a perfume, aftershave or cologne that has a unique smell. Each and every time you are feeling calm, relaxed and at ease, take a sniff of this particular scent. You will quickly learn to associate the smell with feelings of being calm, relaxed and at ease. So, whenever you want to bring back those pleasant, calm feelings, just smell that perfume (or whatever you're using) again and the good feelings will return!

There are many good ways to use this idea. At times when you are anticipating a little anxiety, you could wear that particular perfume or aftershave, thereby allowing the feelings of calm to wash over you.

Step 5: Positive Attention

If you suffer from anxiety, you probably have a tendency to focus on what you do *not* want to happen. You probably also get distracted quite easily, and sometimes find it hard to focus on the task in hand.

If you pay attention to a negative result you want to avoid, you are unwittingly making it more likely that you will achieve that (unwanted) result. However, if you focus on what you *do* want to happen, and what you need to do in order to achieve that result, you are more likely to get there. This is a fairly fundamental aspect of human psychology. You move towards what you are paying attention to. If ever you are giving people instructions, it's much more effective to tell them what you want them to do rather than what you do *not* want them to do. Positive directions work better than ones expressed in the negative.

Here's what to do.

- Deliberately pay attention to what you are thinking about as often as you can.
- Set an alarm if necessary to periodically remind you during the day to focus on what you are thinking.
- Notice if you are paying attention to negative thoughts.
- If you are, stop and think instead about positive thoughts, about what you *want* to happen.
- Also think about what you need to do to achieve this positive result.

(Did this work for you? Becoming aware of your thoughts and feelings is also known as 'mindfulness'. It is a common component in counselling and Cognitive Behavioural Therapy (CBT). Some people need more practice than others, so really use the reminders such as an alarm, or a little note, to help you to practise as much as you need to.)

Summary

- With simple distraction techniques, you can occupy your mind in a way that is incompatible with feeling anxiety.
- Changing your posture by lifting your head, opening your body up, releasing the tension, and doing different things with your hands are all good ways to break anxiety.
- Anxious people have patterns of physical behaviour. If you change the physical behaviour, you reduce or remove the anxiety.
- Use a stimulus with a positive emotion attached, such as a piece of music or a fragrance, to lift your mood.
- Focus on what you *want* to happen, rather than what you do not want to happen. Move towards your positive goal.

In ACT 2, you completed these steps:

Step 3: 'Body And Mind'

Step 4: 'Music Magic'

Step 5: 'Positive Attention'

You're doing well! You won't be surprised to learn that an important part of dealing with anxiety is learning how to relax. But you've probably never learned how to *really* relax, in a way that's so deep and satisfying it's like bliss! This is the subject of ACT 3...

Matt's Story: No More Travel Troubles!

From time to time in this book I'll share some case studies with you. These are all genuine case studies, though names have been changed, and are included here with permission. The stories are told largely in the client's own words, with some editing for space and clarity.

"I work in the construction industry and my job involves a lot of travelling. I have always enjoyed this. One day, however, I started to have panic attacks at the thought of boarding a train or plane. I became anxious, hot, sweaty and short of breath.

This stopped me doing many things that used to come naturally. I was envious of the way other people could travel without a care in the world, while it became a huge ordeal for me.

I wasted thousands of pounds on flights and journeys I couldn't take because of this crippling fear. I became so pre-occupied with the anxiety problem that this in itself became something I worried about. When would it come on? How would I cope and would people notice? The anxiety problem was causing my anxiety!

I tried various ways to deal with the problem but none of them really worked for me. When I got Gary's help, I made really positive strides forward, and through a series of sessions was able, at long last, to deal with what had become a huge issue in my life.

Life's much better now. I rarely suffer from anxiety, and even if I begin to feel some symptoms I am much better equipped to deal with them. I sympathise with anyone who has this sort of problem, it can be really hard to deal with."

– Matt, Construction Professional

Matt is talented, academically strong and focused on achieving his goals. Yet his anxiety made it seem his life was crumbling around him. His anxiety reached the point where almost anything could set it off. He wanted his old life back and I used ACT to help him get it back.

"Nothing in the affairs of men is worthy of great anxiety."

– Plato

*Act 3
Relax
Yourself*

ACT 3: Relax Yourself

Relaxation Matters

It's a very good idea to relax on a regular basis. In fact, it's a good idea to make relaxation one of your regular habits. When you relax, you give both your mind and your body time to repair themselves. This yields significant health benefits. Anxiety and stress, and negative emotions in general, weaken your immune system leaving you more open to illness and disease.

You may well say that this sounds great in theory, and that you would *love* to relax regularly and often, but as someone who suffers from anxiety you have difficulties relaxing. Well, this is what ACT 3 is all about.

ACT 3 will remind your body of its 'reset position', the one where it can remember just what it is like to relax. When I carry out ACT 3 with clients in my hypnotherapy practice, they often say it's the most relaxed feeling they have ever experienced (at least since the start of their anxiety issues).

How To Relax

When you are anxious, your body is 'running hot' — rather like driving a car in first gear all the way with the brake partially on. You make a lot of noise, get nowhere fast, over-heat the engine and wear out the parts of the car very quickly.

To relax you just need to work *with* your body instead of working against it. Your body knows how to relax. Every time you breathe out you relax slightly. Breathing out invokes the body's parasympathetic system, which is responsible for relaxing you.

In the next step I will be using breathing to help you relax. In fact, taking a deep breath and then relaxing as you breathe out can help you at any time. It can give you a nice 'time-out' for your body and mind, and also give you time for thought.

You can amplify this experience by adding a comfortable position, removing distractions, using soothing music, even adding smells that you associate with relaxation. During the process allow your body to adjust appropriately, in order to completely relax.

You may find the voices in your head, the 'chattering monkeys', are a little noisy. If so, just lightly press your tongue up against the roof of your mouth. You should find that the 'chattering monkeys' go silent, or at least seem much quieter and less intrusive. We'll return to these voices, and this tongue-pressing technique, later.

Why Closed Eyes?

During hypnotherapy I often ask people to close their eyes. You may wonder why this is important. Every second you are processing millions of individual pieces of information, which you cross-reference against your memories. Closing your eyes lowers the amount of sensory information coming into your brain and allows it to 'quieten down' a little.

Closing your eyes also cuts out distractions, and helps you to immerse yourself in a step or process. Of course it also helps them relax and therefore they are more able to focus on my instructions.

Also, closing of the eyes also invokes the relaxation response. Some studies have suggested that during blinking your brain activity slows, allowing your mind to process the information that it has been receiving.

So in the relaxation step I will also ask you to open and close your eyes, before finally letting them settle closed. It will help you relax even further.

Step 6: Deep Relaxation

This step enables you to achieve a wonderfully deep state of relaxation. I would not be at all surprised if you found that, by using this step, you feel more calm and relaxed than you have felt for a very long time!

Here's what to do.

- Adjust your position as necessary to get completely comfortable.
- Find a spot on the wall or ceiling in front of you, and allow yourself just to stare at that spot.

5 deep breaths

- Take a deep breath, all the way in. Hold it at the top just for a moment. Then breathe all the way out, allowing your body to relax with it.
- Imagine your body becoming limp and heavy as you breathe out.
- As you breathe out, in your mind say to yourself, "Relax, deeper and deeper, all the way down, just relax now."
- Take a couple of automatic, normal breaths.
- Once again breathe in, hold, breathe out and relax.
- Repeat until you have breathed out and relaxed five times.
- All the time, say, "Relax, deeper and deeper, all the way down, just relax now."
- Let your breathing become automatic, and relax each time you breathe out.

Closing your eyes

- Imagine your eyes getting heavier.
- Allow your heavy eyes to relax and close.
- The moment they close, imagine a wave of relaxation washing through your body and mind.
- Allow your eyes to gently open, then repeat with your eyes getting heavier until they relax and close. Repeat several times, then let your eyes close completely.
- You may find that after repeating this step two or three times your eyes feel so heavy that they just don't want to open. This is absolutely fine!

Heavy arms

- Put your mind into your arms.
- Imagine your arms becoming so relaxed and so heavy that you just can't move them.
- Imagine them becoming so relaxed and getting so heavy that they even start to sink down.
- Continually imagine your arms getting relaxed and heavy.
- Imagine your arms getting heavy automatically, so whenever you exhale your arms relax more and more.

Heavy legs

- Put your mind into your legs and imagine your legs becoming so relaxed and heavy that you just can't move them.
- Continue imagining your legs getting relaxed and heavy.
- Imagine your legs getting heavy automatically, so that every time you exhale your legs relax more and more.

Heavy body

- Put your mind into your body.
- Imagine your body becoming so relaxed and heavy that you just can't move it.
- Continue to imagine your body getting relaxed and heavy.
- Imagine your body getting heavy automatically, so that every time you breathe out your body relaxes more and more.
- Drift and dream...

(Did this work for you? This is quite a long step, so please remember to read it through several times before you carry it out. Practise it several times, and after each time re-read the instructions to ensure that you aren't missing anything out.

Things always get better with deliberate practice. The more times you carry out this step, the deeper you will go and the more relaxed the experience will be.)

If you use this relaxation procedure often, you will develop a relaxation *habit*. You will drop more easily and quickly into a relaxed state whenever you want. You can use this to give yourself a quick 'recharge' of energy at any time, or to help you to drop off to sleep more easily.

Letting yourself drop into a relaxed state will help you get the most out of all the steps in this book. Please remember this. Before you use any of the steps, get yourself into a calm, relaxed state of mind. This really makes a difference.

By practising how to relax you are teaching yourself how to let go of anxiety. You are teaching yourself to be calm and focused on what you want to do. You are strengthening your control of your thoughts, behaviour and actions.

Summary

- Relaxation will give your body a chance to recharge and re-learn how to be calm, which is essential for good health.
- Breathing out and closing your eyes will promote the body's relaxation response.
- Practise relaxing until it becomes a habit.
- You learned how to completely relax your body, which also relaxes your mind.

In ACT 3, you completed this step:

Step 6: 'Deep Relaxation'

So far, you have completed ACTS 1, 2 and 3. You now have the tools and techniques you need to take control of your anxiety at any time.

ACT 4 addresses one very important aspect of anxiety that many people never even realise is part of the problem: the *words* you use every day of your life!

Liz's Story: No More Rage And Sleep Problems!

"I am generally not a worrier, but I did have a couple of issues that were stopping me from progressing with life and work as I wanted to.

The first problem was quite serious. I had split with my partner and he was making things very difficult for me. This led to very strong feelings of anger which began to affect all areas of my life including my family. I was unable to relax and I couldn't sleep even though I was exhausted. For the first time in my life, I was developing a really bad temper.

When I saw Gary, he didn't wave anything shiny in my face or tell me I was getting sleepy, as I had imagined. We just talked.

Gary showed me how to use a visualisation exercise to help me reduce and control my anger. After about two weeks I didn't even need to do that — the issues with my former partner just didn't bother me anymore. I had no feeling at all, no hate or anger.

Gary also helped me with my fear of spiders, which had been a problem from a very early age. Any sight of a spider used to make my heart race and I broke out in a cold sweat. I knew that the spider was harmless, but I felt the fear anyway. After a session with Gary, my fear of spiders receded. I wouldn't say that spiders are my best friends, but I have no problem with them and if I find one I can calmly put it outside the house.

Gary also helped me with sleep. I didn't have a problem getting to sleep but I used to wake up at any time from 2am onwards, start thinking and be unable to go back to sleep. I would then feel tired all day feeling I had not had enough sleep.

After my chat with Gary, sleep is no longer a problem. If I wake up I ask myself if I still feel tired. If I do I go back to sleep and if I don't then I get up and do something. As Gary said, "Who says you need 7-8 hrs of sleep every night?" Sometimes I do and sometimes I don't. Gary has a way of making you question some of the basic ideas in your mind that are causing the problem."

– Liz, Accountant

Elizabeth's chronic anger issues were rooted in anxiety, as I explained in 'Fact File 1'. Her worries and fears were the supporting structure for her anger. When I used ACT to remove the supporting structure of anxiety, the anger simply collapsed.

"Neither comprehension nor learning can take place in an atmosphere of anxiety."

– Rose Kennedy

Act 4
Use
Non-anxious
Language

ACT 4: Use Non-anxious Language

Anxiety And Language

You may not realise it, but you probably use certain language patterns that actually *contribute* to your anxiety issues. In ACT 4 I will explain how these patterns work, and show you how to change them. There is a lot of information here — please take your time!

As you read this section, please take careful note of the language patterns I describe and the mechanisms behind them. Ask yourself whether *you* use some of these patterns on a regular basis. If you are not sure, ask someone who knows you well, or try recording your own conversations and reviewing them. The point is to be become aware of the language patterns you use in everyday speech.

The language you use every day says a great deal about you. Some people wonder whether words drive thoughts or thoughts drive words. I don't really care — all I know is that they are connected. If you change the words you use you change your thoughts. If you change your thoughts you change your behaviour.

Sometimes people dismiss the words they use as 'just a figure of speech' or 'just a saying'. I don't think this is ever true. If you say it, there is a thought behind it.

A word is a unit of sound to which we attach meaning. You hear the sound, and your mind associates it with whatever you have learned is the 'meaning' of that sound. For example, if you hear the sound "cat", I wonder what images and thoughts pop into your mind? You have a reference experience in your mind, a memory, that tells you what the sound means or represents.

Words are associated with thoughts, and the thoughts in your mind often govern the feelings in your body. If you use language patterns associated with anxiety, the associated thought patterns are helping to create, sustain, and possibly increase your anxiety. By using different language patterns, you can learn to avoid this, and to reduce or eliminate anxiety instead.

I am amazed at how much I used to miss before I took a serious interest in language. In my hypnotherapy sessions, I pay attention to every aspect of my client's communication, both verbal and non-verbal (which includes body language, posture, facial micro-expressions and gestures). By doing this, I can often obtain clues and indications that I can use to help my client achieve the results they desire.

The Power Of Certainty

If you suffer from anxiety, you probably experience feelings of uncertainty from time to time. There may often be situations where you feel as if no-one has explained the rules or you have been left unsure about what's happening or what is going to happen. This can be a significant source of nerves and worry. You may also find that this is reflected in the language patterns you use. For example, you may use words and phrases that convey a sense of vagueness or uncertainty. To release yourself from anxiety you need to find certainty.

When I ask a client to grade their anxiety on a scale of 1-10, I get them to be very specific. Clients often come up with vague answers using 'modifiers' such as "I think", "maybe", perhaps", "about" or "I guess". All of these terms indicate uncertainty. If they were certain they would answer directly, "It's a 6". Although at first my client may not feel their anxiety can be graded very precisely, I help and encourage them to come up with a specific value.

There is a very good reason for this. Anxiety stems from uncertainty. If my client doesn't feel certain about what they are experiencing internally (i.e. what grade to give to their sense of anxiety), they won't feel certain about what is going on around them. This is why I help them to come up with a clear, specific number.

I'd like you to do the same. There are times in this book when I ask you to grade your own feelings or evaluate them. Try to be as precise as you can. Each time you catch yourself using a filler or modifier, stop and use a precise answer instead. The more precise and certain you learn to be about yourself, the more of a sense of certainty you can develop about the wider world.

Let me repeat this for emphasis: whenever you catch yourself giving vague answers or using language that is unsure, stop! Replace the vague, uncertain terms with terms that are clear, specific and precise.

Step 7: Avoiding Anxious Language

When you react to any event in your life, you will describe it to yourself in words that become part of how you represent that event to yourself internally. The way you do this, and the words you use, will affect how you assess that event. Some words and ways of expressing yourself will tend to *increase* your level of anxiety. Other ways of expressing yourself will have the opposite effect and make you feel more calm.

For example, people with anxiety tend to use exaggerated language and to make 'mountains out of molehills'. A little 'knock' in the car becomes a 'crash'. I call this catastrophic language. Do you recognise this trait within yourself?

If you use dramatic and catastrophic words, the event or the experience becomes exaggerated in your mind. A small problem becomes distorted and exaggerated so it seems like a major problem. One or two minor setbacks becomes, "Nothing I do ever goes well". A few negative comments from people become, "Everybody thinks I'm a loser."

People with anxiety also tend to take on other people's problems as their own. They see a situation and react as though it were happening to them. An experience they are just *observing* begins to feel like one they are actually *having*. This is misdirected empathy. They see something bad and feel sorry for *themselves* instead of the other person.

People who use catastrophic language often have problems devising good strategies to get what they want out of life. Their perceptions are so distorted and exaggerated that they lose touch with reality. This gives rise to an obvious difficulty. How can you devise good plans to deal with reality if you don't have a very good grip on reality to start with?

I have mentioned that people who suffer from anxiety tend to fear uncertainty, a sense of not being in control. This can leads to 'control freak' behaviour that is very rule-orientated. They feel that by being in control they can manage expectations, manage their experiences, and remove uncertainty. There's nothing wrong with wanting to reduce the amount of uncertainty in life, but they take it to extremes.

Here's what to do.

- Listen to your words and the way you talk.
- Listen out for every time you make a mountain out of a molehill.

Use non-catastrophic language

- Listen out for when you use catastrophic language. Tell your friends to listen out for you too.
- Every time you catch yourself talking in this way – stop!
- Take a reality check. Is it really so bad?
- Is there a less exaggerated way to describe the same thing?
- Change the words you use to that which invoke less exaggerated feelings, e.g. change "crash" to "knock", "disaster" to "small setback".

Specify, don't generalise

- Note when you use sweeping generalisations.
- Avoid generalisations and instead express things in a more realistic way that is also fairer and kinder to yourself. "Everybody hates me". Everybody? There may be one or two people who have said one or two unkind things, but that's not 'everybody' is it? There are other people who like you. "I've never achieved anything". Really? I bet you've achieved a few things here and there, but you're just not giving yourself due credit.

(Did this work for you? You need to learn to notice your own language patterns, and this takes time and practice. Pay close attention to the words you use and how you express yourself. The more aware you become of your language patterns, the better you will become at spotting those times when you use catastrophic language or generalisations.)

Practising Positive Language

Before moving on from ACT 4, I want to mention a couple of good ideas that will help you practise avoiding anxious language and using positive language instead.

Record And Revise

If you want to practise using less wildly exaggerated, catastrophic language, one good tip is to actually record the way you talk, chat and describe things. You can use any sort of voice recorder.

By the way, ignore the fact that your voice sounds different when you listen back to yourself. This happens because you normally hear yourself through the bones of your skull, so of course you will sound a little different on the recording.

When you play your conversations back, listen for any tendency to exaggerate and the use of catastrophic language. Also pay attention to the tone of your voice. The same words spoken with a different tonality can sound very different.

As you play your recordings back you are listening from a different perspective, as if you were someone else. This can help you to listen objectively.

Flip negativity

In the fantasy novel, 'The Hitchhiker's Guide to the Galaxy', by Douglas Adams, there is a character called Marvin the Paranoid Android. Marvin is the ultimate miserable pessimist. His outlook is 'doom and gloom', all the time. He is always miserable, and looking for the worst that can happen.

People who suffer from anxiety often have a tendency to do the same. They use catastrophic language to exaggerate any potential bit of bad news. They take on other people's problems as their own, and tend to look for the negative in any situation. Here are a few examples.

- Students: "I will probably do badly in this exam." "I'll never be able to learn this."

- Work: "This presentation will go wrong." "All my colleagues hate me."
- Social: "They're all looking at me." "I can't talk to her."
- Performance: "It's going to go wrong!", "I can't win."

It could be said that these people are giving themselves a post-hypnotic suggestion for failure. The words you use shape your thoughts, which in turn shape your actions, which in turn govern the results you get. So if you think, "I expect this will go badly," you are in effect directing yourself to that outcome. It would be much better to talk about what you *do* want to happen, and what would be a *good* outcome. You will stand a much better chance of achieving your goals.

Each time you catch yourself speaking in a negative way, flip it around into a positive statement. All you need to do is to listen to your speech, and every time you catch yourself giving a negative, flip it around! Just turn that negative expression into a positive one. "I will probably do badly" becomes, "I'm going to work hard, try my best and get a great result." "I can't win" becomes, "Of course I can win! I reckon I've got the edge over most of these people."

Your mind will move you towards your focus. If you focus on negative results, your mind will take you in that direction. If you focus on what you *want* to happen, you are far more likely to go in the right direction and achieve your goals. The language you use makes a difference. Your brain hears everything you say. If you express negativity, you program yourself to move towards a negative outcome. If you express yourself in a positive way, expressing what you want to happen, you program yourself to move in a positive direction.

Summary

- Words are sounds with meaning attached. Every word, and every language pattern, has a deeper structure of thought behind it. Your learning experience and memories give meaning to the sounds.

- Words indicate the thought patterns, the thought patterns direct actions, and actions direct the results that you get.

- People with anxiety generally use uncertain language patterns that involve fillers and modifiers, catastrophic language and negativity.

- Adopting language patterns that involve certainty, precision, realism and positivity will help to free you from anxiety.

In ACT 4, you completed this step:

Step 7: Avoiding Anxious Language

ACT 5 is also about language, but with a big difference. We're going to look at your *internal* voice, and the dialogues you have with *yourself*.

Naomi's Story: No More Public Speaking Panic!

"I work in Adult Social Care and due to organisational changes I started being asked to deliver presentations on my role.

I have always been shy by nature and the thought of delivering presentations to fellow professionals overwhelmed me with fear and anxiety.

I had real anxiety about public speaking. The very idea made me stammer my words, start to sweat and feel completely fearful.

I decided to contact Gary as I realised that my anxiety of public speaking was starting to rule my working life. If I was to deliver presentations, I needed to at least appear professional if nothing else.

Gary gave me some fantastic coping strategies and visualisation techniques.

I have now delivered my first two-hour presentation, after which I received some very positive feedback from work colleagues.

My working life is much better now. I rarely suffer any anxiety but if I feel any symptoms I know how to cope with them. I hope this book helps and supports people who need to learn how to deal with their anxiety effectively."

– Naomi, Adult Social Care

I had delivered a workshop at Naomi's workplace for her and her colleagues. Afterwards, she booked a private session to help her to resolve some anxiety issues that were holding her back at work. I showed her how to use ACT to allow her career to get back on track.

*Act 5
Change Your
Critical Voice*

ACT 5: Change Your Critical Voice

Your Internal Voice

People often joke that if you talk to yourself, you must be crazy. Nothing could be further from the truth. Everyone talks to themselves to some extent. It is perfectly normal and natural. Every time you express an idea to yourself, you use your internal voice to do so.

Your internal voice develops perfectly naturally as you pass through several stages of learning and language acquisition. At first, as an infant, you just produce sounds. As your brain develops, the specific areas called Broca's and Wernickes develop, which enable you to produce and comprehend language. You start to link sounds with *meaning*, and begin learning how to express yourself with language.

When you are around two years old, you can comprehend more words than you can express. This can lead to a lot of frustration. Some studies have suggested that this is the reason for the behaviour commonly referred to as "the terrible twos". It's the result of the frustration a child experiences because he or she can understand more than they can communicate.

As you continue to grow and develop, you start to understand the link between written squiggles and sounds, and slowly learn to read. At first, you read out loud. Over time, you use less vocalisation until you are just barely moving your lips and you hear the words, as it were, inside your head. You have developed your inner voice and learned to have 'self' talk.

Your Critical Voice

There is nothing inherently wrong with self-talk. It can be very useful and positive. The problems arise when the self-talk is too intrusive or negative. I will refer to this negative, internal voice as your Critical Voice. This Critical Voice may in fact be the main driver of your anxiety.

If you suffer from anxiety, you have probably experienced times when your Critical Voice is over-active and never seems to shut up, filling your head with worries and thoughts of things going wrong (or of things that could go wrong). It's as if your mind is filled with a great many 'chattering monkeys'.

In this section of the book, ACT 5, I will show you how to silence the 'chattering monkeys' any time you want. I will also show you how to modify your Critical Voice and turn it into a *positive* and *supportive* voice instead. These are both very powerful ways to overcome your anxiety.

The Quick Fix

Here's a quick and easy way to temporarily turn off the 'chattering monkeys', or at least greatly reduce them.

Push your tongue firmly yet gently into the roof of your mouth. While you hold it there, notice what happens to your self-talk. You should find that the self-talk becomes greatly reduced. (You can do the same thing by sticking your tongue out and holding it still with your fingers, although this step is perhaps less appropriate in public situations!)

After you have used this technique a few times, you don't even need to *actually* do it — you can just *imagine* doing it. You will find it has the same effect of quietening down the voices.

Why does this work? The areas of the brain responsible for speech and language are linked to the areas that control your lips, jaw and tongue. When you use your internal voice, you may not be saying anything out loud but you still produce micro-movements with your mouth and in your throat. When you stop or alter the micro-movements, you interrupt the self-talk.

In sports performance there are many times where the 'chattering monkeys' detract from concentration and good technique. In golf, negative self-talk is often to blame for poor shots. To be free from distraction while playing a shot, just use the quick fix!

By the way, if you want to speed up your reading, you can use the same trick. Press your tongue against the roof of your mouth to turn off your self-talk. When you read, you 'sub-vocalise' the words you are reading which takes time, slowing down your reading speed. Turn off the sub-vocalisation and you are free to read at a higher speed.

Step 8: CV Change – Sound

Your Critical Voice has its own set of characteristics, such as tonality, pitch and timbre. In your mind, you can change these characteristics. This changes the thought patterns that produce the voice and the resulting physical reactions.

Use this step to modify the qualities or attributes of your Critical Voice (CV). Here's what to do.

- Close your eyes and let yourself become anxious.
- Listen to your Critical Voice.
- Notice the qualities of the Critical Voice: who it sounds like; whether it appears to be from inside or outside your head; its pitch and volume; its distance from you; its speed and so on.
- Change the voice to sound like someone else.
- Move the voice from inside your head to outside, or vice-versa.
- Raise the pitch, and lower the pitch.
- Speed it up, and slow it down.
- Move the voice closer, and move it further away.
- Change the nature of its sound. If it's a rich, deep, booming voice, make it high and squeaky. If it's a rapid, shrill voice, make it soft, weak and soothing.

(Did this work for you? To locate this critical voice, allow yourself to feel anxious and then notice your self-talk. Listen to the words you say, how you say them, and what the voice sounds like. It can help to remove distractions so you can concentrate on your own internal experience.

Use your imagination to assist you with this step. Ask yourself, "What would that voice sound like if..." and change it in any way you want. The more you play with the voice, the more control you will achieve. Start with little steps, and build up from there.)

This step teaches you that you have *control* over your Critical Voice. You can change it, and therefore you can stop it being a problem.

Most people say their Critical Voice is high-pitched and rapid, like the voice of someone in a state of panic and desperation. Try lowering the voice, slowing it down, softening the volume. This reduces the sense of panic.

If you use Step 8, you will end up with a voice that sounds completely different (lower, slower, quieter), so that you can lower your anxiety straight away.

Please repeat this step regularly. If you suffer from anxiety, then you have at some stage developed a skill: to form anxiety. I am helping you to develop a different skill: staying calm, relaxed and in control. Developing a new skill takes practise, and plenty of it. So please practise this step often and enjoy your new control over your Critical Voice.

Pronoun Replacement

Close your eyes and listen to your Critical Voice. Notice which pronoun it uses. Does it say, "I can't do that", or, "You can't do that"?

'I' is internally directed, will probably sound like a version of yourself, and appear to come from inside your head. 'You' is externally directed, usually represents someone else, and often appears to come from outside your head. 'I' is often a tell-tale sign of an anxious person.

Changing the 'I' and 'you' around can make a significant difference. In Step 8, you have already learned how to change the qualities of your Critical Voice. Repeat the same step and this time change the pronoun your Critical Voice uses. This will give you even greater control over your Critical Voice.

You may find it's difficult at first to force this change. Don't give up! The more often you try, the easier it will become. Eventually, it will just start to happen automatically.

Step 9: CV Change – Location

When you experience anxiety, your body tends to move a certain away, adopt certain defensive or protective postures and become more tense. There are many links between feelings of anxiety and the physical movements of your body.

In fact, you have to move your body in order to fully access or experience the feeling. I often use this in my hypnotherapy sessions with my clients. For example, I sometimes ask my client to change places with me. Just by getting up and moving to a different chair, my client has to move and change his or her posture, and this will have an effect on how they feel.

This also applies to your Critical Voice. In this next step, I will ask you to imagine moving your Critical Voice (CV) around, which will change the effect it has on you.

Here's what to do.

- Close your eyes.
- Listen to your Critical Voice.
- If you could see this voice, outside of your head, what would it look like?
- If it were in the room with you, where would it be?
- Use your mind, and move what you see.
- If it is on the left, move it to the right and vice-versa.
- If it is in front of you, move it behind you and vice-versa.
- If it is close, move it away.
- Notice what happens when you move the position of the voice.
- Leave the voice in a place where it is least troublesome.

(Did this work for you? Some people have trouble seeing the voice. However, if you can hear the voice, you can understand its characteristics. As we will see in ACT 6, the Critical Voice will usually look either like a version of you, or someone else you know

such as a family member (perhaps one of your parents) or an authority figure (a teacher you once knew). Listen to the voice and you will hear the tone and the intent behind it. Who and what would that voice look like?

Although the voice is inside your head, for you to imagine seeing who is speaking you have to imagine them being in the room somewhere. So, where would this person be? Use your imagination!)

Every time you make a change to your Critical Voice you are gaining control over it.

I find the next step incredibly effective. It has never failed me in removing anxiety about a future event. I have intentionally saved it until now, because at this point you have become more practised at using the steps and taking control of your own experiences.

Step 10: CV Change – Urgency

Your Critical Voice has good intentions. It wants to protect you, to remove you from a situation that may harm you.

In most people, the Critical Voice speaks very quickly in an excited, urgent voice, driving you to act now! The urgency is fine when there is a *genuine* threat that you need to respond to quickly. However, when the threat is only a perception in your mind, the Critical Voice becomes a nuisance and a problem.

If you experience anxiety that you know is unwarranted, listen to your Critical Voice. Notice the words that you say to yourself, and notice how quickly they flash through your mind. Notice the words that create and sustain your anxiety.

As an example, I have a client who comes to me for help with anxiety when flying. She tells me the anxiety hits her as soon as the plane door closes. She tells me it's as if there's a loud, insistent voice shouting, "*Oh-my-God-I'm-going-to-die!*", followed by strong feelings of panic that are difficult to deal with. When she describes this, the tone of her voice changes. She talks more loudly, and with a great sense of urgency, as she externally expresses what her internal Critical Voice sounds like.

Step 10 plays with the speed, the words, and your internal representation of your Critical Voice. You may find that you just can't get the anxiety back long before you get to the end of the step. Finish it anyway as it will just help to consolidate the changes. (This is an adaptation of an approach I first learnt from the hypnotherapist Nick Kemp.)

(Step 10 continues on the next page >)

Here's what to do.

- Close your eyes.
- Think of an event that makes you anxious.
- Notice the *exact* words that you say to yourself that bring on the anxiety.
- Continue to think of the event that makes you anxious.
- Inside your own mind, say the same words, in the same order, yet very *slowly*, with *long* gaps between them.
- Notice what happens to you during the process.
- At the end open your eyes, then close them again.
- Think of the event that makes you anxious and notice what happens now.
- As you think of the event that makes you anxious, say the words in a *different order*, again *slowly* with *long* gaps between them.
- Notice what happens to you during the process.
- At the end open your eyes, then close them again.
- Think of the event that makes you anxious and notice what happens now.
- See the words you say to yourself floating over the images in your mind.
- See them dissolve, become translucent, evaporating like water on a hot sunny day until they are completely gone.
- At the end open your eyes, then close them again.
- Think of the event that makes you anxious and now notice what happens.

(Did this work for you? If it didn't work for you, you haven't worked with the right words. It's important to notice the exact words you say to yourself.

A client who suffered from claustrophobia told me the words he said to himself were, "I just know that I can't get out and that is what makes me anxious". When I pressed him to identify the precise words his Critical Voice used, he realised they were "I can't get out". Work with the exact words that flash through your mind. Don't be surprised if they contain swear words or profanities.)

Most of you will find this step extremely effective. This one step has solved many people's anxieties, even full-blown panic attacks.

At a neurological level, you will probably find you can learn things more quickly if you learn in 'groups of three', by which I mean trying the same basic step three times and in three different ways. This is what you have now done with regard to your Critical Voice. Before, the way you spoke to yourself was how you accessed the feeling of anxiety. Now that you have changed how you speak to yourself, you cannot access the same anxiety. You may now even find it difficult to access the Critical Voice at all!

Test Yourself

At this stage in a hypnotherapy session I usually get my clients to try and access the feelings of anxiety they had before. They usually find they can't.

I tell them to try harder. I *dare* them to access the old feelings. I *double* dare them! I want them to know *for sure* that they can't get the anxiety back because it is gone and, more importantly, gone for good.

So if you had anxiety, and now it is gone, give it a good test. I know you can remember having the anxiety, and remember what it felt like, but make sure that you can't actually get it back. If you can't, how cool is that?

See if you can access the 'chattering monkeys'. If you can't, great! If you can, don't give up. Go over the steps in this section and practise using them. I am sure you will be successful eventually.

Summary

- Self-talk is a normal part of the way you learn language and speech.
- For a quick fix to quieten the 'chattering monkeys', press your tongue to the roof of your mouth.
- Practise changing and controlling your Critical Voice.
- Practise changing the sound of your Critical Voice.
- Practise swapping the pronouns 'I' and 'you' that your Critical Voice uses.
- Practise visualising your Critical Voice and changing its location.
- Practise slowing down your Critical Voice and making it sound far less urgent.

In ACT 5, you completed these steps:

Step 8: CV Change – Sound

Step 9: CV Change – Location

Step 10: CV Change – Urgency

Your Critical Voice obviously has some strength and power, which is why it could cause so much anxiety (before you learned to control it). In ACT 6, we're going to carry on working with the Critical Voice, but we're going to take this strength and redirect it. As a result, your Critical Voice will become something completely different: a Positive Voice.

Susan's Story: No More Workplace Woes!

"A difficult time in my life left me feeling emotionally out of control. I was finding it difficult to concentrate at work and my anxiety was spiralling out of control. For the first time, I was letting my personal life intrude on my working day. Every morning I was filled with worry and dread about the day ahead.

Luckily for me, my manager arranged for me to see Gary and try the ACT approach. I had no idea what to expect, and was stressed out about even attending my first session, but Gary soon put me at ease. Gary worked with me to control my anxiety, stress and, I suppose, sadness, and I never had to explain or reveal anything that I thought was a bit too personal.

After two sessions I was able to control the panic moments that were causing me so many problems, and to deal with situations that I'd previously found very difficult. Even if some symptoms of anxiety and panic come back in future, I don't fear them because I know how to deal with them. This has made a huge difference to my life. I think anyone with similar problems should realise they don't have to suffer — they can get help, and they can learn to deal with the problem."

– Susan, Legal Professional

This was a slightly unusual case for me. I usually deliver ACT to corporate clients in the form of group workshops aimed at reducing stress in the workplace. Less stress means better performance, happier and more relaxed employees, and a much nicer work environment. In this case, the employer asked me to work individually with Susan. Her boss recognised that she was a valued member of staff who was going through a difficult time, and it was in everyone's best interests to get her the help she needed.

Act 6
Create Your Positive Voice

ACT 6: Create Your Positive Voice

Personality And Voices

Like everyone else, you have many different parts to your personality. The dominant aspects of your personality may be more or less constantly present, while others may only come out in specific situations — at work, at play, spending time with your family. Your internal voices correspond to these different parts of your personality, all of which make you the person you are.

If you suffer from anxiety, one or more of these parts of your personality has learned to have anxiety. This is the part that speaks with your Critical Voice. I want to emphasise that it has *learned* to be this way either through direct experience or by learning from others. The good news is that just as it has learned to be this way, it can learn to be different. This is what ACT 6 is all about.

In the previous section, ACT 5, you learned how to control and modify your Critical Voice so that it wouldn't cause you any more problems. You learned to change its characteristics such as the way it sounds.

In this section, you're going to take this process one stage further and actually change your Critical Voice into something else: a Positive Voice that will actually help you in more or less every aspect of your life. (This is an adaptation and extension of an approach I first learnt from the hypnotherapist Andrew T Austin.)

Step 11: CV Change – Gag It!

Here's what to do.

- Close your eyes.
- Find the Critical Voice.
- If you could see this voice, what would it look like?
- And, if it were in the room with you, where would it be?
- In your mind take some black duct tape, and tape the mouth of the voice tightly shut.
- Notice what happens to the voice.
- Open your eyes, and then close your eyes.
- Now think of the voice and notice what happens.

(Did this work for you? If you can't visualise your voice, go back and re-read the notes I provided after Step 9.

Remember to use your imagination and make things as real as you can in your mind.

If you still hear 'mumbles', then duct tape the mouth a little more tightly and securely. You can use lots of tape, and lots of layers!)

I hope you found this step very effective at turning off your Critical Voice. Have you ever been unable to get to sleep because you feel anxious and the 'chattering monkeys' won't stop? Use this step to switch them off!

Step 12: CV Change – Comfort It!

If you suffer from anxiety, you know that your Critical Voice is strong. It can be loud and dominant, a real force to be reckoned with. Yet its overall aim is to protect you, to remove you from what it perceives to be a threat. It has strength and wants you to feel good. Wouldn't it be good to put that strength to some good purpose? To use it in a positive way for a change?

The next step gets the Critical Voice on your side and gets it working *with* you rather than *against* you.

- Close your eyes.
- Think of your duct-taped Critical Voice.
- Mentally go to that voice and act in a way that *you* would find comforting and reassuring e.g. give it a hug.
- Say, "I know you have your reasons, but what you have been doing hasn't been helping. So right now, please be quiet, and I want you to just relax."
- Notice what happens.

(Did this work for you? Remember that the Critical Voice is part of you, even if it looks like someone else. Be kind to it, really give it some comfort and be sincere when you tell it to relax.)

As you do this step, you are talking to part of your personality. It's part of you. You are talking to yourself, but in a constructive way. You are learning to be different.

When you asked your Critical Voice to relax, and comforted it in a way that you would find comforting, did you notice yourself relax too? This should come as no surprise. What you are working with *is* you, inside your mind.

Let's take it a stage further with the next step.

Step 13: CV Change – Direct It!

Here's what to do.
- Close your eyes.
- Think of your Critical Voice.
- Say to it, "I know you've had your reasons for saying what you say, and you've been quite strong and forceful. I want to direct that strength in a more useful direction."
- Ask it, "Instead of looking to the negative all the time, please focus on the positive and suggest what I need to do in order to get what I want."
- Say, "At all other times please just be quiet, and relax. This is what is safest, healthiest and best for me."
- Carefully take the duct tape off.
- Notice what happens.

(Did this work for you? Be sincere. The Critical Voice has been looking out for you, but it has been doing so in a misguided way that hasn't been very helpful. Mean the words that you say.

If the voice doesn't want to be constructive, then remember that the mind moves towards what it is paying attention to. Remind the voice that it is more effective to move you towards what you want, rather than always trying to move away from what you don't want.)

By using this step as often as necessary, you can get the Critical Voice part of you acting in a constructive way. You have helped it to learn to be different. You have explained how it can play a constructive role in helping you to achieve your overall goals and desires.

There are many ways of working with various parts of your personality, and this is just one of them. Please realise that all the parts of your personality will have a positive outcome in mind for you, even the ones that have given you anxiety!

Negative emotions are there to move you away from something perceived to harm you. A part of your personality that gives you negative emotions is just trying to protect you. Work together with that part of your personality, and allow it to help you achieve the outcome you really want.

Summary

- The voices in your head represent parts of your personality. The Critical Voice is one of these parts, the one that gives rise to anxiety.

- You have learned to listen to the voice and modify its characteristics. You have noticed that when you change these characteristics you change the associated thoughts and behaviour.

- You can also turn off the Critical Voice and can get some peace. While you are enjoying this peace, you can think about how you want the Critical Voice to be supportive and constructive in line with your goals.

- There are many techniques in this section. Gain control of your self-talk and you gain control of your personality. As you gain control you can redirect the strength of your inner voice towards achieving your goals.

In ACT 6, you completed these steps:

Step 11: 'CV Change: Gag It!'

Step 12: 'CV Change: Comfort It!'

Step 13: 'CV Change: Direct It!'

Most people who come to see me about anxiety have been putting up with the problem and 'suffering in silence' for quite some time. There are often issues from the past that need to be dealt with.

This is what ACT 7 is all about: the past, and how to make sure it never creates any problems for you now, in the present.

Anthony's Story: No More Flying Fears!

"I fly two or three times a month on business. I never used to have a problem, but then over a couple of years I slowly developed a real anxiety about flying. I didn't really understand why or how. I used to really enjoy flying, but now I was breaking out into a cold sweat at take-off and clutching on to the arms of my seat. I could feel my stomach churning, especially if we hit a bit of turbulence, and I also had an awful time during the landing.

The problem got worse and worse, until it really started affecting my ability to do my job.

Gary had helped me with a couple of issues before, and so I asked him for help with the problem. All I can say is that it worked, and really quickly. The following week I flew to Copenhagen and it was a totally different experience. I didn't even think about take-off until we were well into the flight. I looked up from my magazine and realised that I wasn't a sweaty, palpitating mess! I was a calm, relaxed air passenger looking forward to an in-flight beer! I wasn't even bothered by the landing. The fear and anxiety have not returned.

I have seen many people who suffer from massive anxiety issues regarding air travel, and all I can say is that Gary's ACT approach was very effective for me."

– Anthony, Marketing Professional

Anthony's anxiety problem was centred on his self-talk. I removed the anxiety of past flights using ACT 7, collapsed the self-talk that gave him anxiety of future flights with ACT 5, and used ACT 8 to 'future pace' good flights in the future.

*Act 7
Escape
Your Past*

ACT 7: Escape Your Past

Healing Emotions

When I present seminars and workshops, I want to build rapport and trust with everyone as quickly as possible. I want them to know that the techniques I use really work. I find the simplest way to do this is with a quick demonstration.

I usually start by asking everyone to think of something from the past that gives rise to a negative emotion when they think about it. Just to be clear, I am not asking them to *remember* having a negative emotion in the past. I am asking to find something that gives rise to a negative emotion *now* when they think about it.

I reassure everyone that I won't ask for any details about this source of anxiety. I then apply one or more of the techniques and interventions that I use in my work. For most people, in *just a couple of minutes* they no longer feel any negative emotions about that particular memory.

In this section I am going to teach you the same techniques, so that you can clear up any negative associations with memories of the past — the ones that promote anxiety.

Programmed By Your Past

Many people feel anxious about something in their past. It can be something they've directly experienced, or observed happen in others.

To take a common example, maybe you were asked to give a speech and it didn't go very well. Maybe you simply messed it up. It's possible you didn't really mess things up at all, or at least not all that badly, but your *perception* is that you really made a terrible mess of things. When you think of that time now, you may get the same anxious feelings.

This is known as 'post-performance' anxiety. It is common amongst performers, particularly actors and musicians. There is nothing wrong with *learning* from the past. This can be very important when you're trying to improve. However, when you *carry* that past experience with you, it's like carrying a heavy burden. This gives rise to two problems.

First of all, this burden from the past makes you feel anxious. Secondly, it means you are effectively preparing yourself for things to go wrong in the future as well. Whatever you pay attention to in your mind becomes what you create in your body. The bad performance from the past becomes your reference material for the future, and this in turn can lead you to *replicate* the past — which is not a good idea.

Any stimulus associated with the bad memory, such as sights, sounds and smells, can trigger the feelings of anxiety. The more often this pattern of 'stimulus and response' is triggered or used, the more established it becomes. The more established it becomes, the more easily it gets triggered by different things. Hence you will find, over time, that more and more different circumstances can lead to the same response and the same feelings of anxiety.

So, how can we deal with this problem?

Step 14: Memory Extension

Close your eyes and think about a happy memory. It can be any memory that gives you a pleasant feeling. Consider how this is represented in your mind. As sight is our dominant sense, it is probably represented via a short mental movie or a still image.

Memories associated with specific events from the past, are termed 'episodic' memories. All episodic memories have a start point, some content and an end point. In the case of a still image, the start, content and end are all at the same point. I want you to recognise the three elements and what they represent.

Whatever triggers the happy memory in your mind provides the start point.

The context and whatever happens during the 'movie', or the principal features of the still image, provide the content.

The end point is usually the point of most significant emotion.

Allow yourself to identify these points.

Notice that as you recall the memory, or run the mental movie, you start to take on the same emotions and feelings you experienced at the time. As I have emphasised many times in this book, what you imagine becomes your reality. This is why you can think of a happy event and laugh again, just as you did at the time of the incident.

If something triggers a *bad* memory, it plays through to the point of most significant emotion and gives rise to bad feelings and unhappy or anxious emotions.

Let me remind you that no matter how bad the past incident may have been, if you are reading this... you came through it! You got through the experience, survived, and moved forward with your life. Wouldn't it be nice to allow yourself to move forward now without that negative burden? This next step will help you to 'move the memory forward' to a happier place.

Here's what to do.

- Close your eyes and think of the troubling memory.
- Notice how you feel.

- Notice the movie you have in your mind, and the end point.
- Add on some time. What happens next?
- Continue adding time to the movie, again and again. What happens next?
- Continue until you reach a safe place in time, where you are happy, safe and having a good experience.
- Notice how you feel now.
- Go back to the start of the movie and run it all the way through to the new end point, where everything is okay and you are having a good experience.
- Repeat twice more.
- Do the same again, but this time twice as quickly.
- Repeat twice more.
- Double the speed again and go all the way through.
- And again, double the speed and go all the way through.
- Now go as fast as you can from start through to end, over and over, repeating it many times.
- Stop and think of that troubling memory.

(Did this work for you? Immerse yourself in the memory and the process. Use Step 6 to relax and remove distractions so you can really concentrate on this step.)

Remember, memories are plastic and you *can* change them. In this step, you took the memory beyond the part that gives rise to negative emotions and followed it through to a part that feels better. This means that the next time you access the memory, it runs all the way through to the good experience. You have removed the problem and left the negativity in the past where it belongs.

Step 15: Deleting Negative Emotion

This next step has a different approach. It leaves the memory intact, but removes the negative emotion associated with it.

Here's what to do.
- Close your eyes and think of the troubling memory.
- Notice the way you feel.
- Now take your left hand and firmly tap your right collarbone, using a steady rhythm, 10 times.
- Stop tapping and hum the first couple of lines of "Happy Birthday", or some other pleasing, cheerful tune of your choice.
- Count from 1 to 10.
- Give yourself a big hug for a second or two.
- Take a deep breath in, hold for a second, then let it go and relax.
- Notice how you feel.
- Repeat as necessary until you can think of the memory and feel either happy about it or at least neutral.

(Did this work for you? Some people feel the tapping, humming and counting is all rather silly. It's okay to think it's silly. Do it anyway! If you don't like 'Happy Birthday' then hum the first couple of lines from any tune that you usually associate with happy thoughts.

You may need to repeat the process several times, and you should experience the feelings diminishing each time. The memory will still be there. You are not getting rid of it, you are just removing any bad feelings that are associated with it.)

This step is based on the brilliant work of neurologist Ronald A. Ruden, who has made a special study of 'tapping' therapies and why they work. The step you have just tried consists of three stages. First, you create a neurological distraction (tapping, humming, and counting). Then you provide a safe place (the hug), and a relaxed feeling (deep breath, let it go and relax). Instead of your memory running through to the point of greatest trauma, it now runs through to a point where you feel safe and relaxed.

Step 16: Fixing The Past

In the last step you learned how to delete the negative emotion associated with a particular memory. However, the memory itself remained the same.

Your memories provide the reference material for your present actions. You may have reference material that gives rise to thoughts like, "I wish I'd done that differently", or, "I wish I hadn't done that".

It's a good idea to change these kinds of memories so that they work *for* you and no longer make you feel anxious.

- Close your eyes and see yourself carrying out the mistake.
- Look at yourself as you run the movie of this memory. See what you look like, see what happens, until the mistake is complete.
- Let the images go completely and blank the screen.
- Now see yourself in the same situation but this time imagine getting things right.
- See yourself in the images doing everything exactly how it should have been done.
- Repeat this movie a further two times.
- Now drop inside your body, see what you would see, hear what you would hear, and feel what you would feel while you go through the action and get everything right.
- Repeat the movie again, this time inside yourself.
- Continue until you get things right, and see, hear and feel how you *should* have done it.
- Repeat this movie a further two times.
- Stop!
- Open your eyes, and close your eyes.
- Think of the mistake and notice what happens now.

(Did this work for you? With clients in my hypnotherapy practice I usually drop them into a nice relaxed state before carrying this out, so they can totally immerse themselves into the experience. You may consider using Step 6 to do the same.

Really make the experience vivid. The more vivid you make it, the more effective this step will be. Sense everything, see every detail, hear every sound and experience all of the feelings.)

Summary

- Anxiety often arises from a past event. When you access the memory of this past event, it gives rise to anxiety and negative thoughts. Any stimulus similar to the one linked with the memory will trigger the same feelings.

- Some people carry bad memories and bad feelings around with them. The bad feelings can be triggered by small incidents. The steps in this section let you modify the memories and leave the negative feelings behind.

- Past experiences provide reference material for how you act in the present. Even though the emotional charge can be removed, you also need to correct any past mistakes so that you don't make them again. The final step in this section was about rewriting the past so you can act better in the future.

In ACT 7 you completed these steps:

Step 14: 'Memory Extension'

Step 15: 'Deleting Negative Emotion'

Step 16: 'Fixing The Past'

Having dealt with the past, the next step, of course, is to take a look at the future. This is the subject of ACT 8...

Jim's Story: No More Sleep Struggles!

"When I first went to see Gary, I was in a very low place mentally. For about eighteen months I had been suffering from chronic insomnia. It was getting to the stage where it was beginning to seriously affect me mentally. I had started suffering serious anxiety issues. It was a struggle to even leave the house, and I had to force myself to go to work completely lacking motivation. I was constantly replaying the same negative dialogue over and over in my head. I decided that this was something I couldn't beat on my own.

In my sessions with Gary he used hypnosis and some of the ACT steps. It felt like a broom sweeping away all my mental baggage and making it so much easier to deal with. That was a year ago. I no longer have any sleep or anxiety issues. As you can imagine, this has made a massive difference to my life."

– Jim, Plumber

Clients who see me about insomnia often say their insomnia is causing them to feel anxious. I often find it's actually the other way around: the anxiety is causing the insomnia. This was the case when I worked with Jim. I used ACT to eliminate the anxiety he was experiencing, and as a result he stopped suffering from insomnia.

*Act 8
Direct
Your Future*

ACT 8: Direct Your Future

Future Memories

In this chapter I will help you to achieve the future that you want, and we'll focus largely on converting uncertainty into certainty.

I have already shown you how your memories affect the way you behave in the present. Your memories provide a lot of reference material that have a direct bearing in how you act and feel.

It's exactly the same with what I will refer to as 'future' memories. I know that sounds a little strange — how can you have a *memory* of something in the future? Well, it's not quite as crazy as it sounds. When I talk about a future memory, I mean a memory that you construct so that it *will* become the reference material for how you act in the future.

When you create a future memory you lay down a path that leads, step by step, to whatever it is you are trying to achieve. At the same time, you are giving yourself information: what you need to do, what you will do, and when it will happen. This takes away uncertainty, and thus reduces (or eliminates) anxiety. That's the theory, and you will *love* how well it works in practice!

When you think about things that are coming up in your life, there may be one or two that make you feel anxious: a sporting event, something you have to do for work, a big social event such as a wedding, and so on. Whatever this forthcoming event may be, you can use the steps in this section to make the anxiety simply melt away.

Step 17: The Day After

For this step, you want as much peace and quiet as possible, so that you can go 'inside yourself', so to speak, and immerse yourself deeply in the experience. Here's what to do.

- Close your eyes.
- Imagine you have just completed your event or task and it has been a great success.
- See yourself the day after.
- See what you look like and notice the expression and emotion on your face.
- What kind of emotion is that emotion?
- Imagine dropping inside your body. See through your eyes, hear through your ears and feel the feelings of being you, the day after everything has gone so well.
- Notice where the feeling is in your body.
- If your feeling had a colour, what colour would it be?
- Make the colour brighter, bolder and more intense.
- Notice which way the feeling is moving.
- Move it faster, as fast as you can.
- Notice the size of the feeling, and make it as large as you possibly can.
- Make it brighter, faster, and bigger until you can't make it any stronger.

(Did this work for you? Some of my clients find it hard to imagine what it would be like the day after a particular event. They often say, "I don't know." I say, "If you did know, what would it be like?" So if at first you can't imagine it, ask yourself what it would be like if you could.

The last part of this step is very similar to Step 2, but instead of removing a feeling we are intensifying it.)

At the end of this step, you are feeling a very strong, positive emotion. This is how you want to feel at the end of whichever task or event you have been thinking about. This is your goal — but you are already experiencing the positive feeling *now*. Feels good, doesn't it? Imagine feeling this way at every stage as you progress towards achieving your goal. Imagine that this feeling just accompanies you automatically every step of the way. That would be good, wouldn't it? In fact, it would be *great*!

You will love how well the next step works. It uses mental rehearsal to construct a future memory that will become your reference point for how to act in the present. As always, the more you practise the stronger the connections will become.

By using this step, you not only feel good, but you know exactly what you need to do in order to achieve a successful outcome. You have removed doubt and uncertainty.

Step 18: From Then To Now

I suggest you learn this particular step in stages. Keep it short and simple at first. Gradually build up the duration and the detail until you can run through the complete step with ease.

- Close your eyes.
- As before, imagine the day after the event, when everything has gone very successfully.
- Experience that feeling of success and achievement.
- Hold on to that feeling. Take a good look at yourself. Notice your posture, your expression and the emotion on your face.
- Take note of that emotion.
- Take yourself back to the event and see yourself performing amazingly well, with great confidence and everything just coming together perfectly.
- Take the time to see yourself performing to the very best of your ability.
- Take yourself back to the period just before the event.
- See yourself perfectly ready and prepared, feeling 100% confident that everything will go just how you want it to (or need it to).
- Take yourself back to the stage just before this; doing everything you did that allowed you to feel so perfectly prepared.
- Take yourself one step further back in time.
- Continue to step back in time all the way to now.

(Did this work for you? The first time that you try this step don't worry about adding too much detail. Just allow yourself to go through the step. Then go back, do it again, and keep adding a bit more detail each time. Repeat this step at least three times, each time adding more details and more feelings.)

Step 19: Mental Rehearsal

The next step builds on the two previous steps in this section. In Step 18, you visualised a successful outcome and all the stages leading up to it. You visualised everything you would need to do in order to reach a successful outcome. This step actually immerses you in the experience so that you don't just *know* what you need to do — you actually *do* it (well, at least in your mind!).

Here's what to do.

- Close your eyes.
- Take yourself to the day after the event and notice everything you can notice.
- Work backwards, through the event, before the event, all the way back to now.
- Run the sequence forward like a movie, all the way through to the day after.
- Repeat at least three times, ending up the day after.
- Drop inside your own body, see through your own eyes, hear through your own ears, and really feel the feelings that you feel the day after everything has gone so well.
- Make that feeling as strong as you can: make the colours brighter, spin the feelings faster, and make them as large and as intense as you can.
- Hold onto those feelings.
- Work backwards through the sequence, experiencing it from inside your own body, from the day after the event to now.
- Still holding on to the positive feelings, move forward through the sequence from now all the way through to the day after the event.
- Repeat at least three times.

(Did this work for you? Some people have trouble holding on to a feeling. To make it easier, once you have the feeling, pinch your thumb and a finger together. This is just to remind you that all the time you have your thumb and a finger together you will unconsciously hold on to that feeling.)

By completing this step, you strengthen and intensify the future memory in your mind.

Whilst you are carrying out this step you are improving your skills. The more times you see yourself performing at your peak, the stronger your skills will be. In sport, mental rehearsal is often the difference between first and second place. The great thing about this is that you can practise, rehearse and improve at anytime, anywhere! All you need is to be able to relax, focus and concentrate.

Step 20: Seeing The Future

For the final step in this section, I want you to think about how anxiety affects your life. I'm not suggesting you *dwell* on it or put yourself in a bad mood! Just think of the times when anxiety or worry has caused problems, or held you back, or made you feel uncomfortable.

Now imagine what overcoming anxiety forever would mean to you. Think about a life where anxiety simply isn't an issue. Imagine how much more you would achieve, and how much happier you would be. (This is an interpretation of the Automatic Imagination Model of Anthony Jacquin and Kevin Sheldrake.)

It's time for the next step. Here's what to do.

- Relax and close your eyes.
- Imagine living your life free from anxiety, worry and stress of any kind.
- Imagine how you *want* to think, feel and behave: always calm, always relaxed and focused, never anxious.
- Imagine being the person you want to be.
- Imagine it completely.
- Continuously imagine all this.
- Continuously imagine all this happening automatically.
- Continuously imagine all this happening automatically, so much that even if you didn't want to, you would still think and behave and live your life exactly how you want to.
- If a voice pops into your head and says this is all just imagination, so it doesn't have much to do with reality, don't worry! Imagine that thought going away, and then carry on happily imagining being the person you are going to be.

(Did this work for you? The more times you do this, and the more detail you add in your imagination, the more successfully you will create complete future memories. By imagining exactly how you want to be, you are becoming that person. You are literally wiring your mind to be this person. Imagination is powerful so use it wisely!)

If you have never tried a step like this before, it may seem a little strange at first and perhaps a bit pointless as well! My clients often ask me what the point is of sitting around imagining things.

The truth is that your imagination is a very powerful tool. It really can be a very useful mechanism for providing focus and shaping behaviour. There's an old saying that, "Where imagination meets belief, the imagination wins every time". I encourage all my clients to use their imagination to the full, and they soon discover how very effective it can be.

If you haven't already completed Step 20, please go back and do it now. In fact, I suggest you use it often.

Step 20 helps you to think about your future and identify a goal or goals. Life is a journey, and I don't want you to wander aimlessly. I want you to know exactly where you want to end up. The more often you run through Step 20, the easier it will be for you to vividly imagine your destination. The more vividly you can see your destination, the easier it becomes to actually get there.

Summary

- Your brain handles 'future memories' just as it handles past memories. The 'future memories' become your reference material, guiding how you will act.
- Repeated mental rehearsal can build up future memories. Whereas before you felt uncertain, you now know exactly what will happen so the anxiety just melts away. You are planning for the future to be the way you want it.
- Each mental rehearsal hones and strengthens your skills.
- Use this step regularly, either for things that make you anxious or for things you already enjoy but want to enjoy even more. These steps are not just for making the bad stuff good — you can also use them to make the good stuff better!

In ACT 8 you completed these steps:

Step 17: 'The Day After'

Step 18: 'From Then To Now'

Step 19: 'Mental Rehearsal'

Step 20: 'Seeing The Future'

If you use all the information in ACTs 1 – 9, you should now be completely free from anxiety, or at least well on the way there. If you don't feel you have completely overcome your anxiety yet, I suggest you try repeating the various steps (paying close attention to the instructions).

I guarantee that you *will* reach the stage where you are totally free from anxiety, enjoying a calmer and more relaxed outlook on life, and confidently planning for a better future.

Anne's Story: No More Spoiled Sport!

"I work as a sports performance coach. I love all forms of exercise. I go to the gym, I do boot camp, I go spinning and I Thai-box. However, ever since I was 13 years old I've had an anxiety problem with running, especially running outside and with other people.

This goes back to my school days and memories of being bullied and judged by other kids. In my adult life, this has led to panic attacks. I would go running and after twenty seconds my head would say "Stop!" over and over. Although my body felt okay, I kept hearing 'Stop!', my lungs felt tighter, then I would panic and stop running. Once I went running with some friends and I had such a scary panic attack it took 45 minutes for me to get my breath back.

Even though I help my own clients with anxiety and mental preparation, I couldn't deal with this on my own. After my session with Gary, dealing with this 'Stop' voice in my head, I felt a lot calmer and able to deal with the problem. Using the steps that he taught me, I was at last able to start running with others and taking part in races. Instead of feeling anxious, I feel excited and in control. Instead of saying 'Stop!' to myself, I hear myself say, 'Come on, you can do it!'.

I have known Gary Turner for 15 years. He is a top sportsman with a vast knowledge of how the mind works. His techniques work and if a particular technique doesn't seem to work for you, he'll find something else that does."

– Anne, Sports Performance Coach

Anne's particular issue involved a deep-rooted anxiety that was preventing her from enjoying running to the full. I was able to help her to clear the issue, so that she could actually enjoy racing and perform to her best. A large part of Anne's problem had to do with negative self-talk that was driving the anxiety. During my session with Anne I mainly used ACTs 5, 6, 7 and 8.

A Simple Request

As we are nearly at the end of the journey, I hope you won't mind if I just take a moment to make a simple request.

If you like this book, and feel it has helped you, please do me a favour and tell other people about it. This would mean a lot to me.

Mention this book to your friends if they, or someone they know, may suffer from anxiety.

Mention it online, and on social media websites. Even a small recommendation from you could lead to someone being able to rid themselves from anxiety forever.

Also, please review the book on Amazon and elsewhere. Good reviews can really make a difference.

By doing this, you'll be helping me of course, but you'll also be helping people who may not already know about the ACT approach and who could really benefit from it.

Finally, you may also want to mention me and my services at your place of work. I deliver ACT workshops for businesses large and small, all over the country. Less stress in the workplace is good for everyone: productivity goes up, sick days go down, and the atmosphere in the workplace becomes just a little more easy-going for everyone.

You can find out more about my one-to-one hypnotherapy sessions, my business workshops and everything else I do by visiting my website:

www.garyturner.co.uk.

Okay, that's enough advertising! It's time to complete the journey...

Act 9
Put It
All Together

ACT 9: Put It All Together!

An Interesting Journey

You have been on an interesting journey (with a little help from me along the way).

You have learned how to control your anxiety, so that you can reduce all the symptoms and in fact eliminate them altogether.

You have learned to silence the 'chattering monkeys' and the Critical Voice that fills you with doubt, nerves and worry.

You have learned how to gain control over troublesome events from the past.

You have learned to bring the future under your control.

Along the way, I hope you have also learned a little more about yourself.

Can you think back to how you were at the start of this journey? The thoughts you used to have and the feelings you used to experience?

Think back to what all those old thoughts, behaviours and actions meant to you. Think of what they stopped you from doing, and in fact how they affected your entire life.

If you learned, used and practised all the steps in this book, you should now be able to live without any trace of anxiety.

Step 21: Put It All Together

We have reached the final step in the book. It brings together all of the techniques and benefits we have seen so far, and tidies up any loose ends.

I'd like you to really concentrate on being who you want to be: the person thinking, acting, behaving the way you want to, and experiencing all the feelings you want to have. Imagine being *that person*, and imagine being that person *completely*.

Think of what it will mean to you to be that person. Think of being in control of your life and being exactly the person you want to be.

Here's what to do.

- Close your eyes.
- Think of every thought, action and behaviour that you want to leave behind.
- Include every time you ever became anxious or felt stressed, and think what it meant to you and what it meant to others.
- As you do this, ask your mind to give you a symbol that represents all of these thoughts, actions and behaviours. This symbol could be a thing, an object, a place... anything at all.
- Allow this symbol to just pop into your head. Don't analyse the symbol. It may not make any logical sense at all, but it doesn't matter.
- Study the symbol intently, becoming aware of every little detail.
- There may also be sounds associated with this symbol, and if so pay close attention to the sounds and study them as well.

(continued... >)

- There may also be feelings associated with the symbol. If so, pay close attention to them and study them.
- You are aware that this symbol represents the past: the way you were, the feelings you want to leave behind.
- Now consider the way you *want* to live. Think about living calmly, confidently and without any symptoms of anxiety at all.
- Ask your mind to change the symbol to one that represents exactly how you want to think, act and behave.
- The symbol may change a little or it may change completely.
- This new symbol represents the new you living your new life.
- Move this new symbol inside your body, into a place that just feels right for you.
- Expand this new version of the symbol so that it fills every part of you, physically, mentally, and if appropriate spiritually.
- Open your eyes.

(Did this work for you? Every client I work with has been able to carry out this step. Don't go looking for a symbol, just allow one to 'pop' into your head!)

This step may seem a little unusual. However, I use it with a great many of my clients and I know that it works very well. It is very powerful, and tends to bring the change process to a very satisfactory conclusion, including taking care of any small and relatively minor details that we may have missed along the way.

Conclusion

Thank you so much for coming on this journey with me. If you have taken your time, and followed each of the steps carefully, your anxiety should now be a thing of the past.

These steps are the same interventions I use with clients in my hypnotherapy sessions. I know that they work, and are firmly rooted in the science of neurology. (Just for the record, they are not the *only* interventions I use. Not every intervention can be simply or adequately conveyed in a book like this.)

This book has been about helping you to overcome anxiety forever. Yet it is also about your journey through life. You took the time and made the effort to do this! Be sure to congratulate yourself and smile about your achievement!

You have learned a great deal about yourself, and how your mind and your body work. You can use this knowledge to your advantage. Now that you have made one major change in your life, defeating anxiety forever, you know that you can change. I wonder what other changes you will make in your life?

I wish you the very best of luck and happiness!

Gary 'Smiler' Turner

Acknowledgements

I would like to thank many of my friends for their assistance in developing this book.

My first thanks have to go to Ian Rowland, the 'Word Wizard'. Ian is a highly experienced professional writer-for-hire. As well as providing me with inspiration and encouragement, Ian has helped me improve every aspect of this book: the clarity of the writing, the flow of ideas, the structure of the chapters and lots more besides. He also guided me through every step of the publication process. Quite simply, without Ian this book would not be here. If you want a writer, or someone who can help you with any writing project, I strongly recommend Ian's services. In my opinion, and that of many other people too, he's the best there is.

I had a long and distinguished sports career during which I developed my own set of mental strategies, some of which are featured in this book. I have received guidance along the way from mentors, coaches and training partners, all of whom became close friends. I want to thank my judo coach Richard Dove for teaching determination and drive, that practice is the most important thing, and to have a sense of humour. I want to thank Tom Mullins for mentoring me not just through my sports but also throughout my adult life. He's the major reason I won so many world titles.

My valued coaches, Steve Fox and Andre Daltrey, have stayed with me throughout my career. I also want to thank my inspirational coaches such as Jesse Saunders and Mick Murphy, as well as my many friends, occasional corner men and training partners. Although there are far too many of you to list here, please know that you all have my sincere thanks and appreciation. If you've helped me at any point along my own journey, or had the pleasure of touching gloves or getting a grip on me, I'm talking about you.

There are many people who have helped me to develop a greater understanding of human psychology, and who have also helped me by providing inspiration, teachings, ideas and discussion. In particular, I'd like to thank Anthony Jacquin,

Adam Eason, Craig Galvin, James Tripp, Alan Whitton, Andrew T. Austin, Nick Kemp, Emma Lovejoy, Michael Perez, Jorgen Rassmussen, Adam Eason, Felix Economakis, Kevin Sheldrake, Joe Stammeijer, Trix Wheeler and Nick Davies, although I am aware there are many others besides. Many of these wonderful people have their own books, products and training courses. I recommend you Google their names and take a look at their work.

I would like to give special thanks to the British Army and in particular the Army School of Physical Training. These fine men and women, who gave me access to their courses despite being a civvie, are the reason why I progressed so quickly in my learning. I would like to thank in particular Dave Garrett, Gareth 'Maz' Maslin, Phil McGregor, Darren 'Daz' Dugan, Carl 'Bennie' Bennett, Jonathan 'Dusty' Miller, David 'Dai' Palmer, Phil 'Babs' Babbington, Kenny Darnton, Graham Carter, Mark Woodhouse, and all the instructors of the PTI's I've trained with.

I would like to thank my family and friends for their support, proof reading, comments and editing during the development of this book. In particular, thanks go to Alex 'Tiny' Gee — your input has been insightful and valued. May I also thank my Mum, Ann Turner as well as Gordon Brown for being great sounding boards, while helping me learn a little about grammar on the way!

I thank my huskies Harley and Max. It is during our daily canicross (cross country running with trained dogs) or bike-joring (being towed behind them on my mountain bike) that I cleared my head, formulated thoughts and planned this book in my mind. I would also like to thank them for being quiet at my feet while I was working, giving me a warm emotion, and not distracting me from my focus.

Of course my biggest thanks have to go to my wife Kirsty for... well, everything!

Recommended Reading

All of these books will help you to understand yourself better. They are all easy to read and enjoy.

Should you wish to learn more about how the human mind works, I wholeheartedly recommend Rita Carter's book, "Mapping the Mind". It is easily the most accessible book I have found that gives accurate and up-to-date knowledge about how the brain works. I also recommend the slightly older book by John Ratey, "A User's Guide to the Brain". For me, these two books made more sense than the majority of psychology texts that I studied. They provide brilliant guidance through the world of neuroscience, and every page is both illuminating and engaging.

Should you wish to learn more about personality, I highly recommend Rita Carter's book, "Multiplicity", which looks into the multiplicity of personality in fine detail.

One of my favourite books is "The Secret Life of Pronouns – What Our Words Say About Us", by James W. Pennebaker. Don't be put off by the title. It is accessible and highly entertaining! You will never be able to listen to someone in the same way again. You will suddenly discover the hidden insights into personality, social relationships, status, leadership, sex, and human nature that are provided by our use of pronouns.

Step 16 uses my adaptation and interpretation of the work of Ronald A. Ruden. I learned a great deal from his marvellous book, "When the Past is Always Present – Emotional Traumatization, Causes, and Cures".

To better understand the mind-body connection from a medical perspective, I strongly recommend Dr Robert Scaer MD's books, "The Body Bears the Burden" and "8 Keys to Brain Body Balance (8 Keys to Mental Health)".

Printed in Great Britain
by Amazon.co.uk, Ltd.,
Marston Gate.